Helping a Child with Nonverbal Learning Disorder or Asperger's Syndrome

A PARENT'S GUIDE

Kathryn Stewart, Ph.D.

New Harbinger Publications, Inc.

Distributed in the U.S.A. by Publishers Group West; in Canada by Raincoast Books; in Great Britain by Airlift Book Company, Ltd.; in South Africa by Real Books, Ltd.; in Australia by Boobook; and in New Zealand by Tandem Press.

Copyright © 2002 by Kathryn Stewart
New Harbinger Publications, Inc.
5674 Shattuck Avenue
Oakland, CA 94609

Cover design by Blue Designs
Edited by Clancy Drake
Text design by Tracy Marie Powell-Carlson

ISBN 1-57224-277-9 Paperback

New Harbinger Publications' Web site address: www.newharbinger.com

04   03   02

10   9   8   7   6   5   4   3   2   1

First printing

Contents

Part III
Now What? Intervention and Program Planning

Preface

I am very grateful for the opportunity to write this book. For the past three years I have been involved with a dedicated group of people working daily on the front lines, as it were, trying to effect change in the lives of the nonverbal learning disability (NLD) and Asperger's syndrome (AS) teens in our care. It is a long journey, involving discovery and failure. This book has allowed me a forum to organize and present the ideas I believe to be true about these disorders. It's possible that, in the years to come, these ideas will form the basis of more profound knowledge; it's also possible they will turn out to be of little importance. Either way, the process is exciting, and my hope for the future of this field great.

As a child psychologist, my work has allowed me the privilege of working with NLD and Asperger's children and their families. Over the years, like many others I have experienced great frustration at the ineffectiveness of my treatment methods with these children. Weekly social skills groups, individual therapy, assessment, and family therapy were helpful, but real change was not often seen. I saw the greatest effect when, acting as an advocate for the child in Individual Education Plan (IEP) meetings, I was able to participate in developing a program at the child's school that allowed the NLD or AS child to succeed. Still, problems were evident and even those successes were limited and disappointing.

In 1998, I was lucky enough to meet and begin working with an incredibly dedicated group of people who shared a vision: to create a program that had as its core the concept of excellent education for NLD and AS students. This program would incorporate many of the ideas presented in this book—not as modifications or adjunct services, but as part and parcel of the educational program. The high school we envisioned, Orion Academy, opened in Moraga, California in September of 2000. At the time of this writing, we have completed our first year, and it has been wonderful and exciting, full of success and surprises and, indeed, some mistakes. I hope this book will allow the reader to benefit from what I have learned so far.

I must tell you straight out that people who are offended by blunt wording or who prefer to find "gentle" ways of describing reality—in other words, those who prefer euphemisms to statements of fact—may find this book difficult to read. I prefer plain talk, and working with this population has only increased my belief that avoiding direct, accurate language serves no purpose. I don't imagine that the parents who will find this book useful are idiots, and I feel I can be most helpful to them by presenting what I think is true.

I may be proven wrong in some of my beliefs, as much is still unknown about both nonverbal learning disability (NLD) and Asperger's syndrome (AS), but I will not avoid directly presenting opinions (mine and those of other authors), as well as general information that is widely accepted. You will see that I use terms like "disorder" and "disability." This is not because I see NLD or Asperger's individuals as less valuable or as having less potential than others. On the contrary, I see the untapped potential that is buried behind attempts to deny the severity of these individuals' problems. As NLD and AS children mature, our refusing to recognize that the words "disorder" and "disability" are starting points for positive change, not ending points that offer no hope, is a sure way to prevent that change. To a person, the many children and teens with whom I worked over the past fifteen years are wonderful individuals struggling with a disability that affects every aspect of their lives in ways that we are only now starting to understand. Our role as the adults who care for them is to support them and to love them, but also to hold them accountable to standards they can, in fact, reach.

I want to thank the many people who have helped me in the process of creating this book—a process that included the successful first year of Orion Academy: Darlene Sweetland, Ph.D., and Kristine Wong, O.T.R. of Orion, both of whom gave me helpful professional feedback along the way; Rosemary Barshop, the true "brains" of Orion; Lawrence Hsu, an Orion student who graciously allowed me to use his poetry in this book; and my dear friend, Ron Rhody, an excellent writer whom I aspire to emulate and who provided a "layperson's" view of the material here. I want to thank the original Board of Orion Academy for their courage and vision—it has been a wonderful first year and it would not have happened without them—Val Simon, Aaron Simon, Gabe Togneri, Jan Etheridge, Donn

Logan, and Judy Lewis ("Webmistress extraordinaire" of the NLDline at www.NLDline.com). I want to particularly thank Catharine Sutker of New Harbinger Publications, who supported this project, finding me after my presentation at the California Psychological Association meeting in the spring of 2000 and suggesting that I write this book. Without her and the people at New Harbinger, the book never would have happened.

I hope you, the readers, find the ideas presented here useful, informative, and engaging enough to incorporate into your work or your family life. I also hope your thinking about NLD and Asperger's is broadened. Most importantly, I hope that someone reading this book will be inspired to join in the work, adding to our collective knowledge of NLD and AS and increasing the effectiveness of our treatment interventions.

Part I

An Overview of Nonverbal Learning Disorder, Asperger's Syndrome, and Related Conditions

1

What Are Nonverbal Learning Disorder and Asperger's Syndrome?

As an infant, Oliver was warm and cuddly. He spent much of his time while awake happily playing with a toy within reach, and he readily sought adults for closeness. He appeared precociously bright, eager to interact, often babbling in response to the vocalizations of others. Sometimes he reacted to loud noises in a frightened or pained manner, and he seemed less interested in bright visual materials than many young children are. As an older infant and a toddler, he often pointed to objects in his world and seemed to delight in the verbal responses of adults who identified the object. He seemed less interested in exploring his world physically (his crawling and walking were slow to develop), but he was clearly interested in what went on around him. His parents were proud of his obvious intellect and they encouraged his exploration of language.

By age three, Oliver had developed quite an extensive vocabulary, although his motor skill development lagged behind that of other children his age. He often complained, using his excellent vocabulary, about the feel of certain articles of clothing: he wanted no tags in his clothes and preferred the feel of only certain fabrics against his skin. Although usually happy and pleasant around his parents, he could fall apart in a panic at times. He would have "meltdowns," crying and screaming at a change of routine, the loss of a treasured object, or the failure of his parents to provide the correct clothing. At times during these meltdowns, he seemed inconsolable and his parents felt helpless to correct a problem they couldn't pin down.

By preschool, it was clear that Oliver was unusual. Although warm and loving at home and generally well behaved, he had few friends at school and rarely engaged in cooperative play. He desired contact with his age-mates, but was clumsy in activities requiring motor skills and had real trouble understanding how to engage a peer in a mutual activity. Other children would ignore him and he was often found playing alone. At home he established a routine that his parents learned well. He developed specific habits that he adhered to. He also developed a special interest in dinosaurs: he was able to name the different dinosaurs with their scientific names, and could identify their correct time periods. It annoyed him, even at age five, that many movies incorrectly portrayed dinosaurs from different periods as coexisting.

NLD and AS: The Invisible Disorders

For most of us, having children allows us to imagine afresh all the possibilities the world has to offer. We wish wonderful things for our children. We arrange our lives and make plans to help them succeed, we dream for them, and, in some cases, we fear for them. But no one who anxiously awaits the arrival of a new family member can imagine the pain, confusion, and turmoil that fill the life of a child with an invisible disorder like nonverbal learning disability (NLD) or Asperger's syndrome (AS).

This book will try to help you lessen your child's pain and confusion, not to mention your own, by offering information, practical ideas, and humor. Knowledge about and understanding of neurobehavioral disorders in children is a new and expanding field. Much of what we know we learned quite recently, and some of what will be presented here is pure speculation, representing the ideas of many people who struggle day to day to improve the lives of these children. The NLD or AS child is an untapped treasure; our work is to learn the code that unlocks that treasure.

What Is a Neurobehavioral Disorder?

A *neurobehavioral disorder* is a neurological dysfunction in the way in which the brain processes information. Such a dysfunction is inherited: it comes with the child. It is not a retardation of any type, but a difference in cognition or thinking that creates difficulties in understanding the world and interacting with others.

There are many types of neurobehavioral disorders; nonverbal learning disability (NLD) and Asperger's syndrome (AS) are but two. Although they are separate diagnoses, these two disorders have some striking similarities in their symptoms, and because there is a definite overlap of successful interventions, it is reasonable to describe them in the same book.

Learning Disabilities in General

The concept of learning disabilities has been around since educators became interested in understanding why apparently bright kids could not perform well in school. A *learning disability* is an inability to learn material and to perform or produce work at a level equal to your potential or intelligence. If a child has a potential well below average, or an IQ measured in the low average range or below, a learning disability would not be involved when that child's performance is below average. In that case, the child would be performing and learning at his or her potential and would not have a learning disability. Children with learning disabilities are by definition bright children—an important point to make to these children when helping them understand their learning needs.

In the 1970s and on into the 1980s, educators, clinicians, and researchers began to focus on language-based learning disabilities. They identified children who were primarily failing in reading or, in some cases, failing in both reading and math. Over time, there was a growing understanding of specific learning disabilities, among them *dyslexia*, or the inability to read. These children became the focus of a concerted effort by researchers, educators, and parents that resulted in the development of many successful programs aimed at remediating these specific learning disabilities. That was almost twenty years ago, and now dyslexia is a well-understood learning disorder with a good prognosis. Today, we find ourselves on the threshold of that same kind of information explosion and program development for children with NLD and AS. In all likelihood, the next five to ten years will see a dramatic shift in the diagnosis and treatment of both NLD and AS.

Nonverbal Learning Disability

Beginning in the late 1960s, researchers began to notice children with specific deficits in social-emotional functioning and poor math skills (Johnson and Myklebust 1971). These children were unlike the traditional learning disabled child in that they did not seem to suffer language-based difficulties, yet they exhibited a consistent cluster of problems all their own. These authors describe a child who is socially inept, and physically clumsy and has difficulty with math and general visual-spatial processing, but can generate language extremely well. From these observations, the first description was published of what would become known as nonverbal learning disability (Myklebust 1975).

Interest in these children continued and in 1989, the first book devoted to NLD was published: *Nonverbal Learning Disability: The Syndrome and the Model* by Byron Rourke. In this book he describes a group of children who have difficulties in five major areas:

- Tactile perception. This is the understanding of how things feel. This understanding includes knowing an object by feel (silk is smooth and pavement rough), but also includes being able to ignore the feel of certain things (the tag in the back of a shirt, for instance).

- Psychomotor coordination. This is the ability to direct actions in a coordinated manner; for example, throwing a baseball into a fishbowl at the local fair to win a goldfish.

- Visual-spatial organization. This involves using visual information (information received from the sense of sight) to know things about the environment; for example, to understand that things that are closer appear larger and things that are farther away appear smaller. To look at a page full of math problems and know where one ends and another begins requires visual-spatial organization. Visual-spatial organization also controls our ability to maneuver around objects in our path when we're walking or running.

- Nonverbal problem solving. Nonverbal problem solving involves skill in knowing how something goes together without having a manual to describe it. Nonverbal problem solving is likely to involve visual-spatial skills and it makes sense that if one area showed poor performance the other would as well.

- Ability to appreciate incongruities and humor. Ability to appreciate incongruities, or things that don't go together, and an appreciation for humor seem to be related skills. The NLD children studied by Rourke had significant difficulties understanding either incongruities or the humor of other people, (Rourke 1989).

The children described by Rourke had well-developed rote verbal skills (accurate, specific use of words), verbal memory skills, and strong auditory linguistic skills (the ability to remember information they heard). This means they are children who memorize information or facts very well, a process called *rote learning*, especially information presented to them verbally. Math facts, spelling words, or a list of baseball statistics could be memorized and repeated easily. These children seemed to remember things they heard, often exceptionally well.

The early researchers speculated that these children suffered from a dysfunction of the right hemisphere of the brain (see figure 1.1). The right hemisphere was considered the source of imaginative thinking, visual-spatial processing, and ideas and thinking that relied on nonverbal understanding of the world. Individuals who demonstrate strong right-hemisphere skills can easily see how something should fit together, not needing verbal or written instructions. In the past, mathematics was considered a right brain activity, as was the ability to read nonverbal social cues, including body language, facial expression, and even tone of voice.

Traditionally, language skills were seen as the domain of the left hemisphere of the brain. But researchers believed that without help or instruction from the right hemisphere, language skills did not include social skills. It was thought that a disorder of the right brain would interfere with the person's ability to "read" social

Figure 1.1 View of the Brain from Above

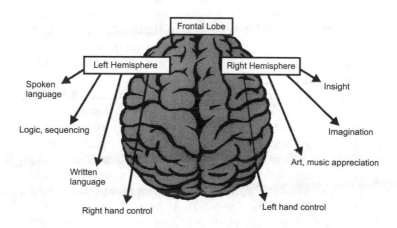

Figure 1.1

situations. Such a person could produce a large volume of language without understanding the social nuances of that language.

The Brain: Current Understanding

Understanding the functioning of the brain as skill sets divided into right and left hemispheres is far too simplistic a view. The brain has layers of connections, from deep within the interior of the brain to the folds on the surface, all serving a purpose. We know now that brain functioning is more plastic (or changeable) and resilient than we thought—early views held that the brain developed by age five and that from then on nothing new occurred. Developments in neurology have begun to map the complex and overlapping functions of different parts of the brain. Learning and thinking in human beings appear not to be limited to one hemisphere. Instead, the many aspects of "learning" cross between the two hemispheres and involve other brain areas.

The central role of the *frontal lobe* (see figure 1.1) has become clearer. Among its many jobs, the frontal lobe is responsible for developing and then supervising the connections between pieces of information stored elsewhere in the brain. One very important job of the frontal lobe seems to be enabling us to learn from new information, in other words, to use novel situations to increase knowledge. Information from both the right and left hemispheres connects with the frontal lobe and, through complex and poorly understood brain actions, humans learn.

Currently, NLD is understood as not simply a failure of functioning of the right hemisphere. The problems experienced by children with NLD in reading social situations, integrating novel information, and learning from experiences suggest a dysfunction of the frontal lobe and the *white matter*—the neural connections *between* the right and left hemispheres of the brain and the frontal lobe. The name "nonverbal learning disability" is actually misleading and unfortunate, as the difficulties experienced are not simply nonverbal, and their scope goes far beyond the problems involved in a learning disability. As you will see in later chapters, children with NLD are not without problems in language. Their problems are not in language production, but in language use. Some professionals working with NLD individuals have suggested that a more appropriate name for the disorder would be "information processing disorder" (IPD, if we stick to the shorthand used for other diagnoses). Yet nonverbal learning disability is the currently agreed upon name that defines the children described here.

How Common Is NLD?

The U.S. Department of Education's *Office of Special Education Annual Report* (1999) reports that 12.8 percent of all children enrolled in school in the U.S. are in special education. Over 8 percent of the children enrolled in school in the U.S. are specifically qualified for special education in areas of learning disabilities and speech and language impairment, two areas where NLD children are often identified. Byron Rourke reports that 10 percent of the children in learning disordered populations are in fact NLD (Rourke 1995). This suggests that approximately 1 percent of the general population of the U.S., or approximately 2.7 million people, currently have NLD. There seems to be no difference in incidence between girls and boys.

Symptom presentation and diagnosis will be discussed in more detail later in this book, but the principal areas of dysfunction in nonverbal learning disability are:

- Deficits in information processing and organizational skills

- Poor visual-spatial and sensory functioning

- Significant impairment of social interactions

At the same time, NLD children generally excel in the following areas:

- Unusual (beyond age level) verbal language production

- Excellent vocabulary

- Good reliance on learning and memory of information that has been heard

Diagnosis of Nonverbal Learning Disability

Nonverbal learning disability is not formally recognized in the most recent edition of the *Diagnostic and Statistical Manual of Mental Disorders*—or DSM-IV, the official guide to diagnosing mental disorders published by the American Psychiatric Association. However, a diagnosis of NLD is usually made by a competent psychologist using a variety of diagnostic tools (see appendix A). The symptom list on page 10 was developed by the author in conjunction with Dr. Darlene Sweetland for screening for NLD. (The version given here has been edited for a general audience.)

NLD and Related Conditions Symptom List

by Kathryn Stewart, Ph.D. and Darlene Sweetland, Ph.D., 2001
For a consideration of nonverbal learning disability expect an 80 percent agreement with the following items:

Social/Emotional Indicators

1. ____ Poor ability to read the facial and behavioral cues of others, especially peers

2. ____ Concrete or literal interpretation of language in social situations; misses the social nuances

3. ____ Excessive concern with the "fairness" of things

4. ____ Very black and white interpretation of rules. Considers rules important in dealing with peers, adults, and learning situations. The child will become upset when a rule is broken.

5. ____ Inconsolableness: once upset, the child finds it difficult to let go of the upset

6. ____ Rigid thinking: once the child has formed an idea about something, he or she does not want to deviate from that idea

7. ____ A diagnosis of obsessive-compulsive disorder made by a psychologist or psychiatrist

8. ____ Proneness to frustration. The child often has *triggers*, or circumstances that feel especially frustrating. These can include hearing certain sounds, sensing pressure to react or interact, or feeling confused about what is being asked of him or her.

9. ____ Sudden outbursts. These are usually intermittent, but have predictable triggers. These outbursts can involve verbalization, physical activity directed at objects, or tantrums.

10. ____ Poor grooming and hygiene. The child (and teen) appears to have no sense of personal presentation, nor of the impact he or she has on others.

11. ____ History of or current sleep difficulties

Language Use

12. ____ No history of language delays. In early development, the child's language developed normally or better than normal.

13. _____ High output of language. The child can sound like a "little professor."

14. _____ Distorted prosody (the rhythm and flow of speech). Many NLD children speak in a monotone voice.

15. _____ Excellent verbal production (a large vocabulary) in a child who performs academically below expectations

16. _____ Problems with pragmatic language (understanding and using language correctly in context; involves understanding the intent of the language) in a child with excellent verbal production. This means children with NLD may not use language as well as they can produce it.

17. _____ Development of expertise in topics of interest, often in a manner that is overly focused on those topics. An NLD child will want to talk at great length about the topic, unaware of the disinterest of the audience. Topics may change over time.

Cognitive or Learning Indicators

18. _____ Inability to pretend

19. _____ Disorganization: although they can be highly perfectionistic, NLD children often cannot organize their thinking, their work, or their routines. They tend to lose assignments, papers, notes.

20. _____ Difficulty learning to tell time

21. _____ Confusion determining right from left. This is often described as *directional confusion*.

22. _____ Deficits in nonrote learning. The child will do better at memorizing facts (rote learning) than at inferring meaning or predicting outcome; the child will have trouble with "What would happen next?"–type questions.

23. _____ Difficulty defining the main idea of a story

24. _____ Dependence on auditory information as support for other learning tasks. The child will often self-talk through difficult activities at home or school or in public.

Sensory-Motor Indicators

25. _____ Tactile sensitivity. The child reports that things "feel funny," and/or has specific preferences for clothing or

blankets with a certain feel. When younger, the child may have wanted all tags cut out of his or her clothes.

26. _____ Auditory sensitivity: sounds bother the child, and he or she has difficulty screening out extra noises. NLD children will often report that people chewing gum or tapping pencils in a classroom or public setting is distracting to them.

27. _____ Tendency to get "lost in space." The child easily disoriented by physical space, actually becoming lost in places he or she has been before. This tendency will be heightened in new or highly stressful situations.

28. _____ Motor skill problems that usually manifest as one or more of the following:

- *Dysgraphia* (the inability to produce written words or symbols, as a result of a brain dysfunction)

- Gross motor difficulties, e.g., problems riding a bike or playing organized sports; tendency to bump into things

- Lack of stamina; easily tired by sports

- Fine motor problems in skills other than writing, e.g., learning to tie shoelaces

Wren's Story

Wren was a cuddly, warm baby when she was being held, but she cried often and had feeding problems as an infant. She was her parent's first child, and they were not concerned that her speech, although developing normally, was focused on certain things. Specifically, Wren had a small pink pony that she had to have with her. This pony was made of silky fabric and she rubbed it on her face and smelled it often. She talked about the toy and about the many horse and pony miniatures she had collected. At age five, she still kept the pink pony with her at all times, even bringing it to school. Her language was developing well; she had a large vocabulary that her parents were proud of. Yet she did not play with other children and did not want anyone except her mother or father to touch her. She was clumsy and couldn't ride a bike or tie her shoes, but she could do almost any puzzle given to her. Her food choices had become more limited and she preferred to have the same thing every day—macaroni and cheese and milk. She often woke during the night, although she denied having bad dreams. Her parents were not concerned; they saw her as shy and imagined that she would grow up to be someone who did not like groups. Her mother and father, both professionals with computer technology careers, had both been shy growing up, and they saw no problem with their daughter's shyness.

Asperger's Syndrome

Asperger's syndrome (AS) has been a recognized, if somewhat ignored, diagnosis since it was first described by Hans Asperger in 1944. The disorder gained prominence and recognition in the U.S. following the published work of Lorna Wing in 1981. Yet it wasn't until the inclusion of AS diagnostic criteria in the DSM-IV (1994) that the disorder began to be studied, discussed, and reviewed with discerning interest. This interest has been partially sparked by the desire to develop an understanding of the overlap between Asperger's syndrome, high functioning autism (HFA), and NLD. According to National Institutes of Health statistics, Asperger's syndrome is described as occurring in 1 in 500 children in the U.S., a higher incidence of occurrence than Down's syndrome or cystic fibrosis (www. N.H.gov 2000).

Common Characteristics
of Asperger's Syndrome

Asperger's children are characterized by normal or accelerated language development in infancy and childhood and a desire to form relationships; yet, similar to NLD children, they often fail in their attempts to socialize. AS children are more likely to have special interests in which they achieve "expert status"; they also show a greater degree of social ineptitude. The areas of special interest often develop into obsessions, and the rigidity of the child's thinking in these areas can be a source of much difficulty.

These children also have excellent vocabularies, even while they fail at the pragmatic or day-to-day use of language. Yet, unlike NLD children, they may do well at certain visual detail tasks (drawing, or seeing a detail that is missing in a drawing or on an object) and certain visual motor tasks (puzzles, copying things, or mazes). The inability to produce written work is a central theme in both disorders. In Asperger's, as opposed to NLD, this difficulty may be less one of dysgraphia (the inability to actually write). Rather, the difficulty in writing is a result of a breakdown in the AS child's ability to turn thoughts into written work. This is actually a processing problem at the level of brain functioning rather than a motor problem with physically producing the letters and words.

Asperger's syndrome has been studied and written about much more than NLD. An excellent book on the topic, written for both professionals and parents, is *Asperger's Syndrome* by Tony Attwood (1997). Attwood's description of the Asperger's childs strengths and weaknesses makes clear the many similarities between Asperger's and NLD. Yet the two disorders are separate and the need for accurate diagnosis is central to effective intervention. Asperger's children are frequently misdiagnosed with autistism or attention deficit disorder, which is similar to NLD.

Diagnosing Asperger's Syndrome

The currently accepted criteria for diagnosing Asperger's syndrome are from the DSM-IV (1994). Having an agreed upon set of criteria for diagnosis allows professionals to maintain a clear and concise dialogue. Without established criteria, it is impossible to know if one doctor's idea of AS is the same as another's.

The major areas for diagnosis AS (according to the DSM-IV) are:

A. Qualitative impairment in social interaction, which includes at least two of the following areas:

- Serious difficulty with nonverbal behaviors such as eye contact, reading and understanding facial expression, body postures, and social gestures

- Problems making friends

- Does not spontaneously want to share enjoyment, interests, or achievements with others

- Lack of social or emotional reciprocity

B. Restricted repetitive and stereotyped patterns of behavior, interest, and activities, with at least one of the following:

- Encompassing preoccupation with one or more restricted interests that are abnormal either in intensity or focus

- Apparently inflexible adherence to specific, nonfunctional routines or rituals

- Stereotyped and repetitive motor mannerisms (e.g., hand or finger flapping or twisting or complex whole body movements)

- A preoccupation with parts of things or objects

C. The disturbance causes clinically significant impairment in social, occupational, or other important areas of functioning

D. There is no clinically significant general delay in language (e.g., single word use by age two years, communicative phrases used by age three)

The Overlap of NLD and Asperger's Syndrome

It has been suggested that NLD and Asperger's are in fact different stops along the same line; that is, that they represent different variations of a similar dysfunction of the brain. There is no question that NLD and Asperger's are not the same disorder. Yet, as both disorders involve similar difficulties processing information and engaging in social interaction, a high level of verbal skills, and a need for a specialized learning environment, I believe that children with these two disorders benefit from many of the same interventions.

All these children display a range of poor social and interactive skills, and they often use language in idiosyncratic ways. NLD children are similar to the Asperger's population in many ways. They have normal to excellent language development, even accelerated development in some cases, but their use of language is perceived by others as "off" or "odd," and although they want to form relationships, they find it hard to negotiate the complications of social interactions.

Asperger's and High Functioning Autism

Some parents and professionals describe Asperger's syndrome as a type of high functioning autism. The idea that Asperger's syndrome is a version of autism is a concept that is highly debatable. To complicate matters, both NLD and Asperger's syndrome are disorders with a wide range of symptoms. Two children with the diagnosis of Asperger's syndrome may not look at all alike. This is hardly good news, either to parents or to the professional community. More research is needed to more clearly define all these disorders, and consistent use of existing diagnostic criteria is required to be sure any two professionals (or parents) are talking about the same type of disorder when they define a child as having Asperger's. Without this consistency, developing a program for the child is difficult, and parents are left to wonder which of all the suggested interventions are really right for their child.

In reviewing the existing diagnostic criteria for Asperger's and autism, the central distinctions between children with Asperger's or NLD and children with autism, even high functioning autism, have to do with language:

Asperger's Syndrome	Nonverbal Learning Disability	High Functioning Autism
Normal language development by age three	Normal language development by age three	Language delay or unusual development by age three
Use language to interact	Use language to interact	Use language to get needs met

Autism is usually diagnosed before the age of five, and the diagnosis of high functioning autism (HFA) is likely to be considered for a child whose early diagnosis was autism and who then progresses (usually through intervention) to develop more normal-appearing language over time. HFA is usually associated with increasing language skill as the child matures and with a higher IQ than is often seen in autism. To further complicate matters, HFA individuals often develop the ability to use that language to interact with the world more effectively than the autistic individual. This leads clinicians and parents to assume that the child who was autistic is now, because of better language use, better diagnosed as having Asperger's. Given that these are separate diagnostic categories, the new diagnosis would not follow logically, yet it is a way of thinking that is all too common.

There is, as yet, little agreement in the field, but some researchers speculate that autism and Asperger's cannot be the same thing, because autism appears to be a dysfunction of the left hemisphere (Dawson et al. 1986) and, as such, is not at all the same neurobehavioral disorder.

Research by Klin, Volkmar, Sparrow, Cicchetti, and Rourke (1995) examining the characteristics of HFA, AS, and NLD finds significant differences between HFA and AS. The authors find significant similarities between characteristics of Asperger's and NLD and find both categories to differ from HFA. They state:

> Finally, regardless of whether or not AS and HFA are truly different diagnostic entities, the significant divergence of neuropsychological profiles suggests that intervention

strategies for AS should be of a different nature, directly addressing specific neuropsychological deficits and building on neuropsychological assets, an approach that has been described as very useful with individuals with Nonverbal Learning Disabilities.

Volkmar and Klin (1998) reported a study they conducted comparing the criteria for diagnosis of NLD and Asperger's. Among other things, they reported finding six areas of deficits in both NLD and Asperger's, and five areas of deficits that neither NLD nor AS children had. These areas are as follows:

Poor Performance

1. Fine motor skills (writing, shoe tying, stringing beads): poor

2. Gross motor skills (bike riding, sports, running, dancing): poor

3. Visual-motor integration (hand to eye activities, such as filling in a bubble on a test score sheet): poor

4. Visual-spatial integration (judging proximity, seeing details, being able to tell foreground from background (e.g., on a map or worksheet): poor

5. Nonverbal concept formation ("seeing" something in your mind, using inspiration, dealing with new ideas): poor

6. Visual memory (remembering things you see): poor

Good Performance

1. Articulation (making the sounds of speech): good

2. Verbal output (talking, producing words in meaningful speech): good

3. Auditory perception (understanding things you hear): good

4. Vocabulary (knowledge of words and word use): good

5. Verbal memosry (remembering things you hear): good

In addition, the authors suggest that HFA is a separate category of dysfunction that is likely to present with deficits *not* found in NLD and Asperger's syndrome—specifically problems using language to develop relationships or connect with other people.

There is no simple answer to this issue, nor is there consensus at this time. As we have seen, the current classification system for disorders, the DSM-IV, includes Asperger's syndrome as an a utism spectrum disorder, while NLD is not included at all. Yet distinguishing among these disorders is important as it affects accurate diagnosis as well as effective treatment. Unfortunately, until we have an agreed upon diagnostic continuum, with clear guidelines for inclusion, confusion about the lines between the categories will remain.

Oliver's Story (Continued)

Oliver entered kindergarten and his parents heard many characterizations of his behavior, ranging from "spoiled" (because of his tantrums and rigid insistence on things being done in a specific manner) to "severely disturbed" (because of his inability to interact socially and his unusual use of language). Parents and teachers alike offered their opinions, many suggesting that Oliver suffered from attention deficit disorder. Oliver's parents, being conscientious people, could not ignore these well-meaning opinions, and they began to have Oliver evaluated by a series of professionals in their community. These professionals suggested stimulant medication and parenting books to "control" Oliver, but his parents saw no positive changes. By the end of kindergarten, Oliver had no friends, continued to use language unsuccessfully as his primary means of interaction, and had received no real intervention for his deficits in visual-spatial processing, motor skills, or social interactions. He had no idea how to "read" another person and continued with his concrete, literal interpretation of language. For example, Oliver's teacher explained his frustration in dealing with Oliver with this story:

> One day, while sitting in a circle with the class, Oliver took a small train from his pocket and began playing with it [Oliver is an expert on trains]. I saw him and told him, "I don't want to see you playing with that again; if I do, I'll have to take it away." Oliver listened politely, then stood up and went to another area of the classroom, where he turned his back and began playing with the train. When I became angry and sent Oliver to the office for being "smart," Oliver had no idea what he had done. As he explained later, "You told me you didn't want to see me playing with that . . . so I moved."

2

Areas of Strength and Weakness

It may seem to parents who are confronting the diagnosis of their child for the first time that all the professionals can see are the "problems" their child has. Parents and professionals alike who spend time with these youngsters know that indeed the deficits are significant and important and should not be ignored. Yet there is more to any individual than his or her problems, and a good assessment will address both strengths and weaknesses. As a group, children with NLD and children with Asperger's have predictable clusters of strengths and weaknesses. Knowing about both allows parents and professionals to more appropriately plan programs and evaluate experiences that will be successful for these children. Each child is unique, and although in general we find the descriptions in this chapter to be true, each individual will have his or her own unique set of abilities, which may or may not include many of the weaknesses and strengths discussed here.

The Good News First: Strengths

As a group, children with NLD and AS are bright, inquisitive learners who nevertheless often perform below expectations in traditional academic settings. The fact that, as a group, these students *want* to learn is a valuable strength. Unfortunately, with repeated experiences of failure, this desire to learn can disappear. As we will see in part II, there are many interconnected reasons these children fail, ranging from specific learning disabilities to inappropriate educational settings and academic expectations. In addition—and this may be a surprise to many—at times the accommodations designed to help these students end up creating a whole series of other problems that in the long run reinforce their "disabled" label.

Michael's Story

Michael is eleven years old, and until sixth grade, he loved to learn. He has poor social skills, or so he is told, although he isn't sure exactly what that means. He doesn't have any friends, and at lunchtime he eats alone. But he does know he can remember anything about World War II fighter planes and can honestly say he enjoys thinking about those planes, looking at pictures of them in books, and talking about them. This past year in school he began to feel that maybe he isn't as smart as his parents keep telling him he is. He can't do the reports his teacher wants and he can't get the homework done and he has trouble with tests—he never can finish in time. He used to feel pretty good about school, but now there is no time for his special interest and the teacher doesn't care about it anyway.

Rote Learning

Some authors have described younger NLD and AS children as excelling at rote learning and memorization of facts (Thompson 1996)—sometimes math or spelling facts or facts relating to a specific area of interest. (Although this is often listed as a strength, the experience I have had is that this skill varies greatly from student to student, and that learning math facts often remains a serious difficulty for NLD children all their lives.) However, the learning of rote information does not mean they can call forth these facts when needed in class, nor does it mean they can use the information in a meaningful manner. In fact, skill in rote learning can become a weakness if teachers and parents do not specifically teach concepts in addition to facts. Reliance on facts, such as memorizing the multiplication tables without understanding the concept behind multiplication, will greatly limit the child's ability to progress in math and, later, in other subjects such as science.

Special Interests

Many NLD and AS children develop a great pleasure in learning facts about a topic of interest. They enjoy this learning activity and will describe it as relaxing. However, although it may be pleasant and relaxing, focusing on this type of activity can cause problems. Let's use as an example a child who memorizes facts about a sports team. The gathering of these facts—reading and rereading, acquiring information from Web sites, magazines, trading cards, or other sources—is ongoing. The child amasses a great number of facts. Yet as the information increases, the child has no internal organizational system—no hierarchy for ordering the information as more or less important. All information is of equal importance, and is thus difficult to use in any meaningful way.

The child, although knowledgeable about the sports team and players, never wants to attend a real sports event. The actual game, the players, the drama and suspense of the sport, are not important. Knowing facts like players' names and statistics about them never translates into an interest in the real players or the real teams. In fact, it may never translate into information for a conversation, because the NLD or AS child only wants to recite the facts he or she knows, not have an exchange of information on the topic. Other people who start a conversation with the child about the sports team, expecting mutual enjoyment of a topic of similar interest, may find themselves disappointed. The NLD or AS child is less interested in dialogue and more interested in an audience, so conversations that turn to this topic become running monologues.

Visual-Motor and Auditory Learning Skills

Asperger's children frequently exhibit skill at puzzles, and may be adept at copying letters or numbers. This visual-motor skill can help them solve problems that are presented to them in a format that taps this strength. An assignment presented as a puzzle, or a vocabulary list presented as a game involving copying or finding the hidden word, may be engaging for the AS child.

NLD children rarely find solving puzzles or copying letters pleasant (and rarely is it a strength), but they often excel at remembering information they hear and respond well to music as a form of relaxation. Vocabulary words presented rhythmically or in brief stories that illustrate meaning will be more helpful to NLD students than any visual copying activity.

Interest in Computers

Both NLD and Asperger's children generally show an interest in computers and appear to be skilled in computer use. This apparent aptitude is similar to these children's appearance of having good language abilities because of their large vocabularies, in that this focus on and attention to computers has led some authors to suggest that NLD and AD children have a "strength" in this area (Thompson

1996). Unfortunately, without careful teaching, these childrens' computer skills often merely reflect their general problems with organization and planning. For example, using a computer to research and write a report can be a great help to any student. Yet while the NLD and AS child may know how to play on the computer, his or her ability to keep notes filed in a meaningful manner, to use information from certain documents in other documents, or just to create an outline of the report, is often limited. The computer becomes another place these children leave confusing and disorganized information, such as files saved in a haphazard manner, never to be found again. Without guidance, NLD and AS children can use computers as just another area for intensive focus without much interpersonal contact. Yet with intervention, their interest in computers can indeed become a strength and a potential career.

Radcliff's Example

Radcliff loves using computers and tries to keep up with the latest developments in wireless systems. As a child, he began learning how to program, starting with simple computer languages and expanding to more complex skills. His ability to focus on one thing to the exclusion of others and to learn a series of actions that he follows precisely helped him land a job with a local computer company. He does the same thing every day—tasks involving specific programming and looking for data. He likes his job and he works independently.

Excellent Language Acquisition

Both NLD and AS children acquire extensive vocabularies early in life. This highly developed language acquisition allows for an entrance into social interaction and academic success. This strength is highly valuable, providing the child with praise and self-esteem and genuine enjoyment. Yet, as discussed earlier, knowledge about language and an interest in facts provided by language are only part of any social interaction. The child who relies too heavily on this one aspect of language use soon meets with social disappointment, and the asset can become a deficit.

When the AS or NLD child is young, between ages three and seven, his or her precocious, "little professor" speech is seen as charming and engaging by adults and is generally ignored by peers. But by age eight or nine, these same peers find this style of speech intrusive and weird. By high school, the NLD or AS child's inability to adopt the flow and rhythm of peer language often leads to isolation and depression. As it is often coupled with the inability to read social cues, the style of language use NLD and AS children rely on for comfort and pleasure actually becomes a barrier between them and their peers. By adulthood, this is usually less of an issue, but there are many years of rejection, isolation, and social failure between third grade and adulthood.

NLD and Asperger's children usually perform well on tests that measure the language they take in and the language they produce. These test scores help us understand their potential for language use, but they do not reflect the children's functional use of language. However, scoring well is often a source of pride for these youngsters, and successes, wherever they occur, need to be supported.

Honesty and Respect for Rules

As a general rule, NLD and Asperger's children don't lie. This is a strength that is often refreshing for teachers and parents. It is not necessarily because these children are morally "better" than other children that they don't often lie. It is most likely a result of their rigid adherence to rules and structure; they wouldn't really consider lying. They are also sensitive souls who are easily hurt by the lies of others, which they experience as incomprehensible actions. The inability to lie can change by the end of middle school, and NLD and Asperger's children clearly are not immune to adolescent pressures. These teens engage in the manipulations of the truth and errors of omission (that is, not telling the whole truth because "you didn't *exactly* ask about that") that are typical of others in their age group.

NLD and AS children learn rules and follow them, expecting others to do the same. In fact, their need for sameness, predictability, and fairness is often a source of conflict with age-mates. But their reliance on rules and predictability and their willingness to play by the rules can in fact be a great strength, as they are trustworthy and reliable and could develop into wonderful employees.

Weaknesses: Not Exactly Bad News

There are three main, interrelated categories or general areas of functional weakness in children with AS or NLD. They are as follows:

- Visual-spatial processing and sensory-motor integration

- Information processing and organizational skills

- Social skills and pragmatic language development

Each of these areas will be discussed in more detail in chapters 4, 5, and 6, and interventions addressing these areas will be presented in part III of this book. For now, a general overview of these areas of dysfunction or weakness is in order.

Visual-Spatial Processing and Sensory-Motor Integration

Visual-spatial skills are the skills that allow you to use visual information to perceive the movement of your body in the world, and to plan and execute that movement. Good visual-spatial skills allow you to judge and manipulate the world and the objects in it using information from your visual field. Examples of visual-spatial skills include the ability to walk a narrow beam, or to run while throwing a ball accurately to another person. These skills require visual discrimination (perception of the differences between things), accurate perception of directions and distances, and coordination of this information with the rest of your body. They require that you note aspects or characteristics of people and things and that you understand what is the same and what is different, using your visual sense and your memories of past experiences.

It sounds complicated, and it is. Yet most of us take these skills for granted. You probably think nothing of the fact that you know the relative sizes of things. When going to pick up a stack of books, you know that they will be heavier than the lunchbox you left sitting there, and you'll adjust your motor movement to account for that difference. You take it for granted that you can find your way from one classroom to another in a large school. For NLD and Asperger's children, the visual-spatial and visual discrimination skills required to accomplish all these activities are often impaired, contributing to a natural clumsiness and frequent experiences of getting lost.

Motor-skills involve the ability to direct your muscles (both large muscle groups and small muscle groups) to carry out actions directed by your brain. This is an area often affected in both NLD and AS children. Normal motor skill abilities develop as part of normal growth, but in the NLD or AS child, these abilities appear impaired from an early age. In the case histories of NLD and AS children, you will often hear that as infants and toddlers, the children did not explore the world primarily through crawling or hand manipulation. Instead, they often preferred learning through verbal exchanges (such as "What's that?" games) with their parents or caretakers. This preference for activities that are not based in motor movement (crawling, running) appears to reflect, in part, a comfort with language-based interactions that seems to remain with these children all their lives.

Motor skills include both *small motor* and *large motor* activities. *Small* (or *fine*) *motor activities* include such things as writing, drawing, cutting, or other finger controlled actions, to name a few. For children with NLD, motor skills that incorporate or use visual information (*visual-motor activities*) are most often impaired. This difficulty with motor activities is often less far-reaching in AS children, as many AS children actually excel in drawing. Both groups of children often experience difficulty with handwriting (including note-taking in class or copying information), or manipulating small parts of things. Perhaps an NLD child holds a fork in an odd manner, or can't seem to spread butter on a biscuit without destroying the biscuit. Drawing is less than pleasurable for many NLD children (though it can be a delight for AS children), and note-taking, tying a shoe, or other visually based fine motor activities have a high failure potential.

Large (or *gross*) *motor activities* include such things as walking, riding a bike, running, dancing, and most team sports or athletic activities. All are similarly difficult for NLD and AS children. Yet some of these children have mastered (and learned to enjoy) large motor skill activities with patient teaching. Though these children need a longer learning period than their age-mates, practice and directed teaching have been successful in helping them acquire skills in this area of weakness.

Visual-spatial processing impacts learning in many ways. NLD and AS students find tasks such as handwriting, note-taking, or filling in forms and worksheets difficult at best, and often impossible. Given these children's difficulties in visual-spatial processing and visual discrimination, these simple tasks are not simple. The problem is not one of failing to understand the task or have the knowledge to complete the task; rather, the problem is that these children have a specific disability that interferes in the processing of visual-motor and visual-spatial information.

Information Processing and Organizational Skills

Processing the many forms of information that you come into contact with each and every day requires many brain functions and complicated communications between brain structures. As we saw in chapter 1, the brain relies on its interconnections to convey information accurately. In people with NLD and AS, this ability is impaired, leaving the affected individual unable to easily or quickly make sense out of day-to-day tasks, like schoolwork, or personal demands, like grooming or relationships. The information goes in, but once it becomes a part of the child's cognitive processes, the child's ability to organize and make sense of and then use or retrieve the information becomes jumbled. It is frustrating for the NLD or AS child and it is frustrating for the parent or teacher of this child as well.

Ari's Story

Ari is a sweet nine-year-old girl who is in a regular third-grade classroom, but who receives resource help two hours a day. She has recently been diagnosed with NLD and her family and school are trying to develop a program to help her. Everyone agrees that Ari is "smart," as she has no problem discussing at length the categories of birds she keeps a log on, nor describing in detail every aspect of the Pokemon card series. She can read above her grade level, yet when the demands of this school year required a report on Native American housing, Ari had no idea what to do. Her teacher sent home a sheet of information, two books, and separate sheets on how to organize a report. Ari's mother sat with her every day after school, succeeding only, it seemed, in provoking Ari to tears and frustration. She found herself feeling the same way. Ari couldn't (or, her mother suspected, wouldn't) write a word. She became totally stumped and unable to proceed when confronted with a blank piece of paper. Her mother became angry and her teacher was confused. Ari could read the material, clearly was listening in class, and could answer questions about Native American homes. Why couldn't she produce any work?

Information Processing Deficits

The case of Ari illustrates the complications and real-life effects of *information processing deficits*. This young girl has taken in and understands all of, if not more than, the information she has been taught on Native American housing structures. The problem is two-fold. First, the information is not organized in any meaningful manner in her memory and second, even information that is organized in some manner cannot be easily called upon by her to produce a coherent written report. In essence, the information goes in, then seems to get lost in a confusing internal filing system. For children like Ari, teachers and parents need to use specific methods that teach not only the information, but also ways to remember and organize what is taught. Given the problems in visual-spatial organization and information processing discussed above, traditional methods of note-taking and outlining using pencil and paper are of little use for these students. Their deficits in information processing underlie a great many of the difficulties these children experience.

Social Skills and Pragmatic Language Development

The third area of weakness, in the development of social skills and *pragmatic language* (practical, day-to-day language that conveys social meaning), is to some degree a result of the two areas of weakness already described. The child's difficulties with information processing, confusion in accurately comprehending the actions of others, and the spatial, motor, and organizational problems described, combine to create pain and anxiety for the child. Social interactions occur on many levels simultaneously, some overt (an obvious message is conveyed, usually through language) and some covert (a hidden message is conveyed, usually via tone, inflection of verbal language or body language, innuendo or implied meaning). NLD and AS children do not understand these multilevel communications and miss the social cues and implied meanings that others understand.

For example, an NLD or AS child will not understand the social convention of personal space without being directly taught to stand the appropriate distance from others when interacting with them. The child will not implicitly understand the differences in personal space that depend on degrees of relationship; for example, that you stand closer to a close friend than to an acquaintance, and that you maintain a respectful distance when dealing with your principal or teacher.

These children interpret language literally, often missing sarcasm, humor, or even threats. The facial expressions and changes in tone of voice that convey the meaning in such statements are missed by these children, who rely on the literal meaning of the words to understand the communication. These misinterpretations of language may be humorous, but they can also create painful and confusing social experiences.

One girl was told by her mother, on the morning of her fifteenth birthday, that her birthday was a special day and she could "do whatever she wanted today." When she arrived at school that day, she had, unbeknownst to her mother, helped herself to a large amount of candy. She had a terrible day at school. In two of her morning classes, she became upset and disruptive when her work was corrected (something that was quite unusual for her). When questioned following the second episode, she finally stated, in an offhand manner, that it was her birthday and that her mother had told her she could do whatever she wanted. She took her mother's statement from the morning literally ("It's your birthday and you can do whatever you want"), and was upset and confused that her work was not accepted as it was, since it was the way she wanted it to be.

The Perspective of Another Person and Pragmatic Language

In general, most NLD and AS children and teens experience great difficulty seeing another person's perspective. This difficulty appears as a failure of empathy, a self-centered worldview that often makes them seem robotlike and cold. This is not the case; NLD and AS children desire close relationships with others and feel extremely sad, even falling into depression, when their relationships fail to develop.

A central focus of any intervention program must be on teaching pragmatic language, self-observation, and the ability to adopt another person's perspective. Traditionally, NLD and Asperger's children have participated in pragmatic language training programs—usually in a small group run by a certified speech therapist. These groups, similar to social skills groups run by licensed psychologists, focus on developing the child's ability to use language appropriately and develop behaviors that are socially acceptable. The children's success while in the group is usually high, and the experience is a valuable one. Yet most professionals find that the skills developed in the group do not generalize easily outside the group. It is a problem worth further study.

Pragmatic Language Screening

We use the following questionnaire at the Orion Academy. Developed from a form used at Pathways Academy at McLean Hospital in Boston, this review is used to evaluate an entering student's current pragmatic language levels; it is then used again over the years to measure improvement. Students eventually learn to rate themselves and come to participate in the development of their pragmatic language skills. Development of useful measures of progress in these skills is another area in need of continued research.

Pragmatic Language Skills Review

Next to each statement, please write the number that best describes the frequency of the behavior:

1 = almost always
2 = usually
3 = about half the time
4 = rarely
5 = almost never

Nonverbal Communication

_____ 1. Looks at the eyes of person speaking with

_____ 2. Uses facial expressions appropriate to content of words

_____ 3. Understands the facial expressions of others and responds appropriately

_____ 4. Understands the emotions of others and responds appropriately

_____ 5. Recognizes nonverbal cues and gestures (body language)

_____ 6. Acts at an age-appropriate level

_____ 7. Recognizes the spatial relationship between people or objects and self: stands the appropriate distances from others; has sense of size/weight of things

_____ 8. Refrains from making inappropriate noises

Expressive Skills

_____ 1. Speaks clearly (does not mumble)

_____ 2. Speaks with varied and appropriate tone and volume

_____ 3. Is able to take another person's perspective

_____ 4. Does not ramble on one topic, as if unaware of other's interest

_____ 5. Understands sarcasm

_____ 6. Understands and uses metaphor appropriately

_____ 7. Can let go of an argument, even if the other person does not agree

_____ 8. Understands own internal state and can respond to inquiries about self with more than "I don't know"

Conversational Skills—Topic Maintenance

_____ 1. Chooses a topic appropriate to setting

_____ 2. Introduces and discusses topic clearly

_____ 3. Expresses *relevant* information and expresses it *concisely*

_____ 4. Maintains a topic in conversation

_____ 5. Changes topics appropriately

_____ 6. Understands how to tailor conversation to audience—e.g., peers versus teachers

Conversational Skills—Turn Taking

_____ 1. Takes turns in conversation—does not monopolize

_____ 2. Attends to listener's comprehension and attention to what he/she is saying

_____ 3. Is appropriate when interrupting both peers and adults

_____ 4. Waits to be called on or acknowledged before speaking in class or a group

_____ 5. Appropriately asks a speaker to clarify comments made

_____ 6. Is flexible when there is a change in topic

Speech Conventions

_____ 1. Introduces self appropriately to others

_____ 2. Uses appropriate conversational pleasantries (greetings, apologies, responses to others)

_____ 3. Makes him/herself available for conversation (is approachable)

_____ 4. Talks "to" people, not "at" them

_____ 5. Asks for help when needed

_____ 6. Initiates original (nonredundant) conversation

Peer Skills

_____ 1. Establishes and maintains appropriate friendships

_____ 2. Refrains from making fun of others

_____ 3. Welcomes others to join group

_____ 4. Offers and accepts criticism appropriately

_____ 5. Offers and accepts compliments appropriately

_____ 6. Uses appropriate slang with peers

_____ 7. Demonstrates empathy

_____ 8. Seems confident in same and opposite sex interactions

_____ 9. Responds to verbal conflicts appropriately

_____ 10. Compromises and negotiates appropriately

_____ 11. Can let another "win" argument

_____ 12. Listens to another person's perspective without having to impose own

Other

_____ 1. Recognizes and expresses own emotions

_____ 2. Does not blame others for own issues or feelings

_____ 3. Demonstrates remorse when appropriate

_____ 4. Assertively deals with peer pressure

_____ 5. Respects the hierarchy of a school or other setting

_____ 6. Cares what others think of him/her

_____ 7. Can understand the purpose of rules, even when doesn't agree

Although it was designed for use in a specific school setting, Orion's pragmatic language skills review is a tool that can be used by parents and professionals who know the child well. It allows parents and professionals to understand the complexity of the language skills we all use on a day-to-day basis. Further, the review sheet provides a way to evaluate the current skill level of a child and to reevaluate the child as the school year progresses, allowing parents and teachers to target areas of specific difficulty. Without some way to assess a child's social language skills and progress, it often feels like the development of pragmatic language skills is both difficult and mysterious. The review shows that, though it may be a slow and difficult process, it is not a mystery. The development of pragmatic language skills can occur in any child, and the involvement of the school and the family is central to the process. A tool such as the review sheet offered here is one way to increase understanding between the family and school, involving both in the support of the child.

3

Why Is It Important to Understand the Child with Nonverbal Learning Disability or Asperger's Syndrome?

A child born with nonverbal learning disability or Asperger's syndrome is not the child most parents expected. These children's needs often defy definition and parents feelings of helplessness and inadequacy can increase with each passing year. This charming, loving young person seems impossible to predict at times, cannot achieve in areas other children find easy (bike riding, shoe tying, participating in birthday parties, turning in completed homework assignments), and struggles with worries and fears that parents find difficult to understand.

These children are also not the students expected by most school districts. Neither traditionally learning disabled nor classically gifted, they present a challenge teachers and schools are rarely prepared for. Many fall into the unusual category of *gifted learning disabled* (which is not the contradiction in terms it appears to be). But as the NLD or AS child gets older, the "gifted" part of his or her learning disability seems less helpful. The language skills that the child relies on are not enough as the need for social skills and more complex information processing come to the fore. The NLD or AS child experiences school as more and more confusing and frustrating. For most of these children, the third grade marks a decline that they can not seem to reverse alone. The social pressures increase—everyone isn't as accepting as in first and second grade—and the academic challenges increase dramatically.

In third grade, classrooms across the country begin to expect integration of information as part of the learning process. In addition, textbooks in many places purposely ask questions or present problems in ways different from the way they were taught. This educational trend can cause problems for NLD and AS children even earlier than third grade. For example, consider a child struggling in the first grade with the math concept of place value. In the classroom and on the practice sheet, she has been using the word "groups": "Put these apples into *groups* of ten. How many *groups* of ten do you have?" Yet on the worksheet sent home for homework, the child is confronted with problems that ask her to put the items into "sets." She is unable to do the worksheet and her teacher is confused about how she could have "forgotten" this concept, when that exact day she could do it in class.

Obviously, she has not forgotten it. The word "sets" does not mean the same thing to her as "groups" and thus she has no idea what is being asked of her. As we will see, her significant learning disability in processing information and rigidity of thinking contributes to her perceived failure. Although this example is a problem of classroom materials and methods for a first-grader with a learning challenge, it also represents a real problem for the child to conquer. The world will present all children with unique situations where they need to apply their knowledge in a novel manner—something that will not come easily to the NLD or Asperger's child.

Program Needs

As a parent, you will need to become knowledgeable about NLD or AS—not only so you understand your child's challenges and can thus help address them, but also because, ultimately, it will fall to you to become the advocate for your child. This will be so unless or until schools across the country recognize the great needs and vast potential of these children and begin providing an education that benefits them. As the previous chapters have suggested, such an education will need to include programming in the NLD or AS child's areas of weaknesses:

1. Visual-spatial processing and sensory-motor integration

2. Information processing and organizational skills

3. Social skills and Pragmatic Language Development.

Attention Deficit Disorder

Most school districts and, unfortunately, many uninformed professionals often misunderstand and misdiagnose the needs of NLD and AS students. The most common error describes these children as having attention deficit disorder (another neurocognitive disorder). Attention deficit disorder actually occupies more than one diagnostic category in the DSM-IV. The major categories NLD or Asperger's children are misdiagnosed in are either AD/HD-HI (attention deficit disorder—hyperactive type) or AD/HD-I (attention deficit disorder—inattentive type). The criteria for a diagnosis of attention deficit disorder are shown in table 3.1. The issues of distractibility, impulsivity, and poor concentration are central to this diagnosis.

Although it is possible to have a dual diagnosis (that is, a child may have both NLD or AS *and* AD/HD), this is not necessarily the case even when it has been suggested to a parent. In young children, NLD and AS often appear with symptoms similar to those of AD/HD—concentration problems, impulsivity, and distractibility. But those very symptoms are also part and parcel of NLD and AS.

In some ways, an attention deficit functions in a neuropsychological disorder like a fever functions in a medical disorder. The fever in and of itself only indicates a problem in the body. Similarly, a deficit of attention really only describes the overt problem the child is struggling with. A fever can point to many things, from spinal meningitis to a simple cold. What a difference correct diagnosis makes, as the treatment for a cold is not the treatment for meningitis. Similarly, the problems that confront the AS or NLD child are important to understand and diagnose correctly, because what is special and also problematic about NLD and about Asperger's syndrome is not the same as what is at issue with attention deficit disorder, and these disorders needs to be understood separately.

Impulsivity

Impulsivity is a tendency toward sudden action on a thought or idea, without consideration of the effect that action might have. In NLD and Asperger's, the impulsivity often displayed by these children is the result of a rigid thinking style that requires reaction to stimuli presented. The need to react to the stimuli is experienced as immediate, with no delay mechanism, or "buffer zone," if you will, before thought becomes action. For example, someone in the class mentions baseball, and the impulsive child hops out of her seat and gets the baseball from her backpack to throw around the class, never thinking it will get her in trouble.

Table 3.1:
Diagnosis of Attention Deficit Disorder

Attention deficit symptoms are present in early childhood, are behaviors that are persistent, and occur in many settings (not just at home or at school). These symptoms have been evident for at least six months, are inconsistent with the development level, and are causing significant impairment in social, academic, or occupational functioning. Onset of the symptoms occurs before age seven.

There are three categories of attention deficit disorders:

AD/HD—Inattentive (AD/HD-I)

- Does not appear to be listening
- Cannot sustain attention once he or she begins—in tasks or in play
- Makes careless mistakes and/or fails to pay attention to details
- Has trouble organizing self and activities
- Has trouble following through with assignments or tasks
- Avoids tasks with multiple steps or requiring sustained effort
- Easily distracted by outside stimuli (clocks ticking, people talking)
- Forgets what he or she is supposed to be doing
- Loses things—books, pencils, keys, toys

AD/HD—hyperactive, impulsive (AD/HD-HI)

- Fidgets or squirms, can't sit still
- Often appears to be "on the go"
- Runs around or climbs on things excessively
- Blurts out answers without being called on
- Talks excessively
- Has trouble waiting to take turns
- Interrupts or intrudes in conversation
- Seems to never be quiet
- Has trouble working alone

AD/HD—combined (AD/HD-C)

- Has characteristics of both sets of criteria

NLD and Asperger's children are most likely to engage in verbal impulsivity. The verbal impulsivity teachers see so often in these children usually involves blurting out the answer to a question (right or wrong) without waiting to be called on. Other verbal forms of impulsivity are also part of the compulsive behaviors some of these children experience. A child might find himself repeating a word in a rhyme sequence, impulsively indulging in a string of nonsense words he finds funny. For example, the vocabulary word is *orange*, and the child repeats *orange*, then proceeds to say *lorange, forange, porange, sorange*, and on and on. Needless to say, others do not find this very funny.

Distractibility

Distractibility is simply the tendency toward becoming distracted—shifting attention from what you were supposed to be focusing on. While you are driving, it is distracting to answer a cell phone call. Some people can actually manage to maintain attention on more than one thing at a time. Unfortunately, for NLD and Asperger's children and teens this is not usually the case. In NLD and Asperger's children, distractibility appears to be due to heightened sensitivity to stimuli (smell, sound, feel) or to a ruminative thought stuck in the child's head. Distractibility is evident when a child looks to the clock whenever it ticks, or stares at another child, unable to get back on task because that child is tapping a pencil. These children's difficulty with concentration stems from the culmination of all the deficits we have mentioned, combined with the anxiety that these children try to deal with on a day-to-day basis. Try paying attention to a teacher who is talking about long division when you hear the child next to you tapping a pencil, the clock ticking, and the hum of the heater—all while you try to tune out the recurring thoughts in your head about Pokemon (which you actually prefer to think about) and arrange your body at a desk that causes you to lean forward in an uncomfortable position. Most adults would be hard pressed to stay focused on the lesson.

Anxiety Disorders

Anxiety is a feeling of worry or fear that can occur at any time, often for no apparent reason. During most of human evolution, anxiety was necessary for survival. The early human who experienced a sense of anxiety and was careful when hearing the growls of a saber-toothed tiger was more likely to survive (and less likely to be lunch) than the human who had no sense of what to be anxious about. When normal anxiety no longer functions to warn us and provide a way of accurately judging the safety of our environment, that anxiety can become the source of a disorder.

Michael's Story

Michael is twelve years old, the second of four children in his family, and seems larger than other children his age. People often mistake him for older—his size and his excellent language skills probably contribute to this common error. Yet Michael hides a secret from peers and adults at school, at temple, and at family gatherings that include anyone but his immediate family. Michael is always worried about germs. The idea of people coughing, sneezing, or breathing on food or utensils makes it almost impossible for him to eat in public. He pretends to eat so people will leave him alone, but he rarely puts anything into his mouth. He feels an overwhelming need to wash his hands when someone sneezes or coughs, and he finds himself in the bathroom more than normal—sometimes three or four times in an hour. He parents know about his worry and tell him it's "silly," that he should ignore the sounds of others and push those thoughts out of his head. He would if he could, but the thoughts and the sounds intrude anyway. He also finds it difficult to stand too close to people. He's not sure why (and it isn't always the germ worry), but he just feels "funny" when there are lots of people close around him. Sometimes his heart beats faster and he worries he'll have a heart attack. He never has, of course, and knows it is a "silly" thought, but sometimes in public places crowded with people he still worries it will happen.

Obsessive-Compulsive Disorder (OCD)

Many NLD and AS children suffer an anxiety disorder at some point in their lives; many experience symptoms of obsessive-compulsive disorder (OCD). *Obsessive-compulsive disorder* is one of the anxiety disorders identified in the DSM-IV. It is a disorder that can occur at any time in a person's life, but it is not unusual in children, as earlier clinicians thought. The disorder is characterized by the presence of both obsessions and compulsions to a degree that causes distress for the individual and interferes with some aspect of his or her life—personal, professional, or academic. Normal, reasonable worries and fears are not the concerns in this disorder.

Obsessions

Obsessions are thoughts, ideas, or images in the mind that occur over and over and create for the child a sense that he or she cannot control them. These thoughts appear without warning, and once they occur, the child cannot easily get them out of his or her mind. Some common examples are obsessive thoughts about germs, about being contaminated, or about having an accident on the road. The visual images that accompany many obsessions can involve violent or sexually focused material and are disturbing and distracting to the individual. Needless to say, it is hard for the child to have obsessive thoughts, and perhaps even harder for the parent when the child begins to describe these thoughts. But in no way does the presence of intrusive thoughts or obsessions mean the child will act on these thoughts. Many a parent has worried that the fact that their child thinks these things (e.g., imagines his teacher with blood running down her face) means he will do them. There is no evidence this will follow. In fact, obsessive-compulsive children are generally less violent and more frightened than most other children are.

Compulsions

Compulsions are the actions that the OCD child feels compelled to perform as a result of his or her obsessions. They are actions these children "need" to perform over and over again; for example, washing hands after touching a doorknob. Compulsions often have a number associated with them—for example, a certain number of times that an action MUST be performed to prevent some disaster from happening. Many times the child does not know exactly what the disaster will be; he or she just has an overwhelming bad feeling. The compulsive ritual that develops can take over the child's life: it can take hours to perform, interfering with the child's day-to-day functioning.

Ryan's Story

Now fourteen, Ryan started compulsively washing his hands when he was ten years old. At school or in public places, he had to wash and dry his hands repeatedly (six times, to be exact) before he could leave the bathroom. No one knew about it; he would try to go to the bathroom without others noticing how often he went, and when that didn't work, he carried prepackaged hand towelettes (his mother was impressed with this, especially since most other boys his age didn't seem to care about cleanliness). Ryan wore long-sleeved shirts as often as possible, and he developed a trick of slipping his hand inside the sleeve, using the fabric to cover his hand so he could open doors in public places. The problem really only came to light when his parents noticed that the toilet was clogged over and over again: Ryan used too much toilet paper (again, to keep his hands clean).

Linda's Story

Linda was an excellent student, getting grades that never went below a B. In the middle of sixth grade she began to worry more and more about being able to maintain her academic prowess. Without knowing when it started, she found herself involved in a thinking ritual that she felt she *had* to do to avoid getting a poor grade on a test. This ritual consisted of thinking of every "bad" grade she could get, in order, without allowing a positive thought to intervene. It went like this, "I'll get an F, I'll get a D, I'm sure of it, I'll get a C." If the thought that she might get an A or a B slipped in, or if she was interrupted in this thinking series, she had to start again. As time went by, she began engaging in these thinking rituals about all her worries, especially about the safety of her mother and father. Finally, her grades began to suffer, and her daily life was disrupted by the amount of time it took her to complete these rituals.

Treating Children with OCD

Needless to say, treatment of OCD is essential if the afflicted child is to be able to function in any school program. Most children with OCD respond very well to the standard treatments—usually a combination of medication to lessen the symptoms while the child completes a course of cognitive behavioral therapy (CBT). John March, M.D., has cowritten an excellent book describing the treatment of children with OCD (March and Mulle 1998). Any parent whose child has developed symptoms of OCD, with or without NLD or Asperger's syndrome, should seek a competent evaluation and treatment for the child. Early intervention is more likely to be successful, and for children, many of whom do not require continued medication, the tools of CBT are effective throughout their lives. In children with NLD or Asperger's who are also diagnosed with OCD or AD/HD, the NLD or AS is the central disorder. This distinction may seem like hairsplitting—what difference does it make if the child has one diagnosis or the other or, more to the point, what difference does it make if they have both? The incorrect diagnosis of an NLD or AS child will result in inappropriate treatment and classroom placement. For example, NLD and AS children are frequently diagnosed early in life as having AD/HD. This is usually a result of their problems with on-task behavior, attention, and concentration. The problem with this error can be significant, as an NLD or AS child is not dealing with the same issues as a child with AD/HD. Placement of NLD and AS children in classrooms with AD/HD children whose behavioral problems are central and who respond best to behavior modification and stimulant medication is a serious mistake. Although medication can be helpful for some NLD children and many Asperger's children, behavior modification techniques and classroom settings with AD/HD children are not useful options. AS and NLD children's particular pragmatic social needs are ignored under this approach, and the anxiety they feel usually increases in these settings. Further, their visual-spatial difficulties remain untouched in favor of controlling their behavior.

School District Diagnosis versus Clinical Diagnosis

Since the passage of Public Law 94-142 in 1976, school districts across the country are required to provide special education services to students whose disability "prevents them from benefitting from their education." Yet many states have added to and otherwise modified the original law, so parents need to be knowledgeable about the laws for their particular state. Every school district also has a unique and specific set of guidelines for inclusion in special education programs. The department of education in each state can help parents get accurate information about the laws in their area.

It is important to remember that the language of the professional medical and mental health communities is not the same as that of the educational community. School districts use categories and labels that may sound like the labels and diagnoses in the DSM-IV, but they do not necessarily mean the same thing. The DSM-IV has no diagnosis for NLD, nor does it have "behavior disorder" as a diagnosis—although school districts may use that category. Similarly, school districts often refer to a student as severely emotionally disturbed (SED); this is not a DSM-IV diagnosis. Qualifying a child for special education services under the category SED usually reflects a decision by a group of people, including the parents, about the types of services that will likely benefit the child.

It becomes confusing for parents as the different systems talk about their child using different language—or, worse, language that sounds the same but has different meanings. Parents must not only learn to decode the world of the NLD or Asperger's child; they must also learn the language of the systems they will now interact with. At times, this interaction may require the help of education attorneys and other professional advocates.

The Need for Continued Education on NLD and AS

It is essential that parents and education professionals become informed about nonverbal learning disability and Asperger's syndrome. If the adults around them lack the knowledge to evaluate services, plan programs, and provide a safe learning environment for these children, their future looks bleak. Without the right diagnosis, incorrect services may be put in place, sometimes setting a child back years. The NLD or Asperger's child may be placed in a classroom with children whose needs are both severe and opposite to his or her needs. The last thing an NLD or Asperger's child needs is to be placed in a classroom with students with behavioral problems of any kind. Nor should he or she be placed with children of limited intellect or language-based learning disorders.

In the right environment these children's special talents overshadow their challenges, and it is through continued learning and study into these disorders that we can develop successful learning environments for them. With appropriate services and planning, our NLD and AS children can look forward to a future as bright and full of possibilities as anyone could wish for them.

Part II

The Effects of Nonverbal Learning Disability and Asperger's Syndrome

4

Speaking a Different Language: Social Skill Development and Social and Emotional Functioning

As we saw in previous chapters, nonverbal learning disability and Asperger's syndrome affect three main areas of functioning:

1. Social skills and Pragmatic Language Development

2. Visual-spatial processing and sensory-motor integration

3. Information processing and organizational skills

This chapter and the next two will discuss the effects NLD and AS have on each of these areas.

Where the System Breaks Down

If one area most dramatically sets our nonverbal learning disability and Asperger's syndrome children and teens apart from their peers it is in the area of social and emotional functioning. These children experience difficulties in reading subtle social cues and understanding day-to-day social conventions. They don't really understand how to fit in or be "cool." They have trouble understanding how others feel, or learning to be flexible in how they present themselves to others. They seem to have missed out on developing coping strategies for the complexities of peer interactions. In short, the NLD or AS child's system of social functioning doesn't run as smoothly as most people's, and it is most likely to break down in the following three areas:

1. Failure in the use of pragmatic language (practical, day-to-day language disorder)

2. Failure to understand and utilize the interactive quality of language—these children use language to tell others things or carry on a monologue, not to interact. They also experience significant difficulty understanding and sending appropriate social cues using voice sound and tone, body language, humor, and innuendo or implied meaning.

3. Failure in the ability to simultaneously track multiple levels of social interactions: that is, keeping track of tone of voice, body posture and gestures, and facial expression as well as the actual meaning of the words conveyed.

NLD and AS children generally desire relationships; they form close attachments to their families and often have a naiveté about them that adults find endearing—though their peers can tease them relentlessly about it. Indeed, these children's social and emotional dysfunction affects every aspect of their lives and, if left untreated, is usually the reason they fail to make a transition to a separate and meaningful life outside the family. In short, the social skill dysfunction is among the most serious issues confronting these children, and it is probably the most difficult to successfully overcome.

A Word about Teasing

Teasing becomes the central torment of most NLD and AS children's lives. Teasing is the most often cited reason parents seek new programs for their children. While most NLD and AS children and teens appear normal in most physical aspects, their peers *know* they are different and react to this difference. This reaction from others combined with the NLD or AS child's limited repertoire of responses often sparks escalating unpleasant interactions. These children's incredibly poor social skills, and their desire to use language as a solution to their problems and a cover when they are uncomfortable, make for a bad mix with other kids. Every one of the many children I have worked with complains about being teased and dreams of a place where he or she can be accepted and can make friends. Unable to find a way out of the cycle of being teased, they usually withdraw into increased depression and isolation. Early attempts to fight back by engaging their peers in verbal exchanges are usually glaringly unsuccessful, adding confusion and humiliation to the mix. Eventually, NLD and Asperger's children find themselves on the periphery of social events, ever circling, never involved.

Learning to Cope

Although the stories these children tell are heartrending, it is important not to overreact and remove them from all contacts that might prove to be unpleasant. It is not enough to protect these children from insensitive peers, moving them to safe and controlled environments. Such an intervention has a place and can be an appropriate part of an overall plan. But protecting the child though manipulation of the environment is not enough. NLD and AS children must learn coping skills and, even more important, must come to understand their part in social interactions if they are ever to make the friendships and working relationships they desire. They will never be able to control other people—only themselves. This alone is a hard lesson for these children and teens, who often see control, logic, and "fairness" as the basis of all interactions. But the rest of the world may not see life as they do. The sooner they learn ways they can change *their* part of an interaction, the sooner they will be successful in the world. Their particular disabilities clearly impact this particular learning; as we have seen, these children have a very hard time understanding the complexities involved in social interactions, and they have an even harder time understanding how *they* contribute to their social problems. A focus on creating change in several areas of language and social behavior will be necessary to improve the child's ability to interact and to cope with others.

Andi's Story

Andi is a ten-year-old girl who is a fourth-grader at a local public school. She tries very hard in her class and wants to have friends, but finds that the other girls talk and laugh and seem to have a secret language she doesn't understand. When she tries to talk to them about a book she is reading or about cats, a favorite subject of hers, they listen politely for a few minutes and then start talking about something else. She has tried telling them more about cats or her books, in the hopes of interesting them with her knowledge, but it doesn't seem to work. Often, they walk away from her, and no one seeks her out to talk to or play with. Teachers and students notice Andi's monotone style of speech, but no one knows what to say about that—and Andi has no idea what they mean when people try to describe it to her.

Failure in the Use of Language

Failure in the use of language can be observed in NLD and AS children in their failure to make language work for them in social situations. For example, consider this situation: Mrs. Wong (the classroom teacher) has asked Sue (an NLD fourth-grader) to be in charge of the coveted red bouncy ball at recess. Sue, not really understanding the potential for social status presented to her here, will likely respond by giving the ball to whomever asks for it first. Instead of including herself in the play and becoming part of the group of children, she is likely to hover and worry, keeping track of the "rules" for use of the ball. Without help, she is unlikely to know how to organize any play with the ball, not to mention how to keep herself involved at all. As we will discuss later in this book, NLD and AS children may not be adept at sports or activities using gross and fine motor skills, but with direction and help they can be central to the play—as referees, organizers, and keepers of the scores. The key is in helping them learn how to turn a deficit into an asset.

How Do These Children Use Language?

Language is a comfort for these children and teens. They rely on language, even hiding in their words at times. They tend to produce a lot of language, but it fails to work for them in a number of important ways.

- They produce language that is accurate but not functional. This language conveys information but fails to establish connections between the children and others. They understand the content of the words but often miss the emotional implications language can have.

- It is as if they miss the potential for emotional impact their words can have on others, although they feel the impact others' words have on them.

- They talk *at* people, not *with* them. This behavior is a direct result of their inability to realize that language is a way of interacting, not just lecturing. A monologue on whether an ion cloud has a circle shape or an oval shape may be interesting to your science teacher, but to other adolescents it is boring and pedantic.

- They fail to understand the *nuances* of language, focusing on concrete interpretations of what others say. An example in an earlier chapter illustrates this problem: Oliver understands the teacher's message that he "does not want to see" the toy he is playing with as a message to remove the toy from the teacher's line of sight, rather than to put it away, as was implied by the teacher's statement. Another example is that of the fifteen-year-old who interpreted her mother's statement that she could do "whatever she wanted" on her birthday as literal permission.

- They have difficulty with *sarcasm or humor*, since humor often relies on tone and inflection of speech for its effect. This problem makes negotiating the social hierarchy of middle school or high school almost impossible for many of these children.

- Their *prosody*, or the tone and rhythm of their speech, is often significantly "off." Again, they have trouble with the subtleties that make language more than an act of speaking, and they fail to understand that how you say something can be as important as what you say. Take the phrase "Mrs. Lee, do you want me to read this book now?" Where you put the inflection conveys as much as the literal meaning of the words. Here are a few examples:

"Mrs. Lee, DO you want me to read this book now?" (I can't believe you really do.)

"Mrs. Lee, do you want ME to read this book now?" (Not ME, you must mean that other kid over there.)

"Mrs. Lee, do you want me to read THIS BOOK now?" (Not this book, you must mean another book.)

"Mrs. Lee, do you want me to read this book NOW?" (What? NOW?)

There are more possible inflections, but the point is clear: each sentence, although it contains the same words, does not have exactly the same meaning as any others. In fact, a couple of these statements, if said in the manner suggested, would appear rude to a teacher or other adult in authority. The NLD or Asperger's child has not learned the subtleties and nuances of the differences presented here, and would need these examples explained.

- Their good memory ability may actually be a detriment in social situations, as these children tend to rely on rote fact. When in a stressful situation (as almost all social situations are for the NLD or Asperger's child), they will tend to talk about something that makes them comfortable. This is likely to be an area of special interest or knowledge they have spent time learning about. It is also likely to be something unusual or very detailed. Unfortunately, this response can worsen the social situation, as peers and others around will usually find the conversation boring and lose interest in continuing the interaction. The NLD or AS child has a difficult time understanding that his or her audience has lost interest in the topic. Teenage peers may also make sarcastic comments, or ignore the NLD or AS teen, which is hard for the NLD or AS teen to understand. By the same token, these children do not make very good listeners when someone else has a topic that they themselves are not interested in. They usually need specific and direct teaching on how to engage in the give-and-take of appropriate social conversation.

Failure to Understand the Interactive Quality of Language

Failure to understand and utilize the interactive qualities of language may be in many ways the single most devastating "disruption" that results from NLD, AS, and related conditions. A growing body of literature on concept of theory of mind (including Nicholas Humphrey's 1984 book, *Theory of Mind*), along with a variety of clinical experience, suggests that the inability to adopt another person's perspective underlies the majority of the social difficulties these children experience. They fail to recognize the point of view of others, or to even realize that others *have* a point of view that influences their behavior. It follows that they don't realize that what they do affects the thinking—and thus the behavior—of others. They don't really know that others even experience feeling about them (except for the most demonstrative forms of anger or joy). This failure occurs at the most basic level of human interactions, the connectedness we feel with each other.

How Relationships Form

The ability to have meaningful relationships with others is based in part on shared experiences—a sense that you and the other person are of like mind, are "one." This connected feeling develops early in life through normal interactions, with no direct teaching. Language helps form this sense of social connectedness, but most of us experience it long before we have acquired spoken language. For normally developing young children, much is conveyed in body gesture, facial expression, and eye gaze. Even children too young to talk will point and look at an object, directing their caregiver to look in that direction. This nonverbal direction involves a complicated series of interactions, and has as a basic premise the child's understanding that both he or she and the other person are *thinking*—and thinking about the *same thing*. It is an amazing and complicated process, and it's also something we take for granted every day. Not so for NLD and AS kids. This skill is something they never really master and, as a result, all their advanced language skills fail to allow them into this secret club of mind reading—for to them such nonverbal communication must seem like a psychic ability.

Theory of the Mind

Simon Baron-Cohen's excellent essay, *Mindblindness* (1995), discusses at length the concept of *theory of mind*, which involves the common human ability to "mind read." Of course what he describes isn't *really* mind reading (as in the late-night advertisements for psychic help). Instead, it is the ability most people develop to share thoughts and to have a good idea when others are thinking about the same things they are. This ability manifests itself when we follow the line of a conversation or read a gaze or gesture and assume that we share ideas about what things mean. For example, we assume that when we describe something as "red," the other person holds in his or her mind the same idea of red as we do. Indeed, if the other person is color-blind, this would not be true, so there are times when our assumption about shared thinking is incorrect.

Theory of mind allows us to hold in our minds a full range of mental representations—"dog" is a specific mental representation; "car" is a different mental representation. Further, and in many ways more importantly, theory of mind also comprises our ability to develop a "theory" about thinking. This means we understand that other people believe or think things; this understanding is a must if one is to decode social behavior in any useful or meaningful manner.

We see theory of mind operating in the ability to:

- Pretend

- Understand what a dream is

- Apply beliefs to understanding emotions

- Distinguish appearance (what something looks like) from reality (what something is)

- Introspect (demonstrate an awareness of one's own thought)

- Develop the executive function (disengage from current action, to change or formulate plans, or take action on those plans)

- Integrate information

Children who do not develop these skills will have to be directly taught to understand the feelings and beliefs of others, learning socially appropriate responses along the way. These individuals include NLD and many AS children.

The failure of NLD and AS individuals to understand the interactive qualities of language can be understood as a deficiency in their theory of mind—they cannot "mind read." We see the effects of that disability in many ways, a number of which we have touched on, and further described in the paragraphs that follow.

- When they engage others in conversation, these children's narratives are often disjointed, out of context, superficial, or otherwise confusing. But they know just what they mean, and have difficulty appreciating that others do not understand what they are referring to.

- These children tend to have areas of interest or idiosyncratic focus—these are often called "enthusiasms." The child will often launch into a monologue on the subject, and is not likely to notice that his or her listener has lost interest in the topic.

- As mentioned before, these children's tone of voice is often bland and monotone. This may be a result of the fact that they lack the concept that the listener may be *interested*, and that they could make their speech sound *interesting*. In effect, they are not speaking for or to the other person, but more to themselves, and the idea of keeping someone interested is a new concept.

- These children never really understand the concept of pretending. They are unlikely to engage in a lot of fantasy play or "pretending" as young children, especially when pretending involves engaging others in the fantasy. To engage in mutual pretend play would be very difficult for these kids as it requires a shared imagining, a thinking together.

- Often, the NLD or AS child experiences a failure in the ability to distinguish appearance (what something looks like) from reality (what something is). This inability creates confusion in them and at times is the basis for their social naiveté.

- In some cases the child will have difficulty recognizing someone they have met many times before, especially if the child meets the person in a different setting than usual. The private psychologist for one of our students was visiting the school, and when the student happened by, his doctor said hello to him by name. The student turned to his doctor and said, "Who are you?"

- Often, the NLD or AS child or teen experiences difficulty with introspection—looking inward at the self. Although these kids have the language to describe the inner world of their thoughts and feelings, they often do not have an awareness of this world. Even with direct teaching, the NLD or AS child will only slowly learn the nuances of his or her inner experiences.

- NLD and AS children have significant difficulty understanding social cues. Given their inability to adopt another person's perspective or to think about how they affect others, it is no surprise that NLD and AS children have trouble socially. Understanding the meaning of other people's behavior is quite a task when you must work without the tools the rest of us were so easily given.

An intact theory of mind involves much more than just forming connections with others. It involves complicated mental processes that can be seen working in many crucial social behaviors and skills.

Joint Attention Behaviors

Children, even before the development of language, will direct the attention of their caretakers with the direction of their gaze. The caretakers *monitor the gaze* of the child and the child monitors the gaze of the adult—this means each is aware of what the other is looking at. As motor skills increase, the child will add pointing as a means of directing the visual attention of others. These *joint attention behaviors* are not taught; they develop naturally. Here's an example of how joint attention behaviors work:

1. The child sees some balloons and points towards them.

2. The caretaker looks in the direction the child points, "mind reading" the intent of the child, which is to direct his or her gaze toward an object.

This example illustrates a *showing behavior* which involves showing things to others—in essence, sharing the experience of looking at an object. Children who do not engage in joint attention behaviors such as gaze monitoring or showing behaviors probably have not developed the essential internal mental concept of the connectedness between themselves, their caregiver, and a desired third object (the balloon in the example just given). This internal concept (or set of concepts) helps form the foundation of intuition, a necessary part of "mind reading," as Dr. Baron-Cohen calls it—the power to quickly know things about others or related to others without rationally thinking them through. Most children with NLD or AS understand the idea of "seeing" or "looking," but not the idea of "knowing" in the sense of intuition. The experience of knowing something implies an internal, nonverbal intuitive sense and is often difficult to define. The NLD or AS child has significant trouble with this concept.

Predicting the Actions of Others

In practical terms, if you don't understand what others are thinking about, and that they think about you, you cannot predict their actions. You have no idea how to affect another person's behavior. It makes the world feel random and frightening. It makes every encounter a potentially novel experience—and remember that these children suffer a disruption in their ability to integrate information (or learn) from novel situations. As we have seen, it is likely this is a real dysfunction of the brain. The rest of us learn from past experiences, building up our banks of social knowledge. These children don't, and their experience of social interactions must feel overwhelming and unpredictable. It probably feels like everyone speaks a language they don't understand and can't seem to learn. That experience of the world is likely to contribute to these kids' reliance on their own ordering systems—odd or compulsive as they may be.

Predicting the Emotions of Others

Studies of the ability to predict emotion in others (versus the ability to only recognize emotion in others) have suggested that a child must understand the causes of emotions in order to predict them. The child must also have some theory about the beliefs held by the other person in order to understand what that person's emotions are. This (predicting emotions) is a complex skill, and one that appears to be lacking in many NLD and Asperger's children. The consequence of this lack is easy to imagine: without the ability to predict the emotions of others, every social encounter would be a novel experience, an experience where you would have no idea what to expect.

Failure in the Ability to Simultaneously Track Multiple Levels of Social Interactions

Most of us take for granted that we can keep track of the content of a conversation, the body language and tone of voice of the speaker, and our own reaction to what is being said, all at the same time. Yet if any of these abilities were missing, imagine the many ways a simple conversation could go wrong. Now imagine the effect on our social acceptance if most of our conversations continued to go wrong. That is the reality for NLD and Asperger's children. As we saw earlier, the NLD or AS child or teen is likely to have difficulty reading the facial expression or tone of voice of others. He or she will likely focus on concrete interpretation of the language of the speaker. This concrete or literal interpretation is what the NLD or AS child is most comfortable tracking, but it not always what the other person means. The NLD or AS individual has no way of gauging that he or she has missed the point. When stressed, the NLD or AS individual is likely to rely on what he or she knows—language—continuing to talk whether the other person is interested or not. Interactions go from bad to worse as the NLD or AS individual becomes confused and frustrated, starts talking more, and experiences ridicule or rejection from the other person. Eventually, these children withdraw from any social situation they can, and their skills diminish further.

Adolescence: A Final Note

When these kids enter adolescence and attempt to deal with the complications of adolescent social structures, they don't have a chance. The NLD or AS teen is unlikely to come prepared with the knowledge of and experience with social interactions and "mind reading" that everyone else has. These teens' point of view is self-focused, and their inability to adopt the perspective of another person helps make them totally unaware of the rules of social conduct.

Yet these teens are capable of learning the rules, and the earlier they begin the better. And even though they have NLD or AS, they still need to learn the same lessons in life that their peers do—some easy, some hard. To allow an NLD or AS teen to grow into adulthood unprepared for the expectations of adult life is truly to abandon him or her to a harsh reality. In many ways the lessons of social community are some of the most important lessons to be learned. These lessons, hard as they may be, must be part of any educational program that helps the NLD or Asperger's teen develop his or her special talents and become a functioning member of the adult community.

5

Lost in Space: Visual-Spatial Processing and Sensory Integration

NLD and AS individuals have difficulty knowing the limits and extent of their physical self in the world. It is as if they are not completely aware of where their body begins and ends. This disruption of perception is particularly acute in the areas of visual-spatial processing and sensory integration.

Visual-Spatial Problems

As noted in chapter 2, visual-spatial processing is the ability to use information from the visual field to understand the world around you. Visual-spatial processing deficits affect how information gained through the visual field makes it into memory. For many people, remembering things they see is easier than remembering things they hear. Yet for NLD and AS children, information gained through the visual field is less likely to make it into memory, as visual-spatial processing deficits interfere. Information gained through auditory channels—listening—is more likely to make it into memory.

Visual-spatial processing problems also appear to greatly affect fine and gross motor skills, including writing, sports skills, balance, and coordination. It is unclear why this is so, although sometime in the future medical science may discover the reason NLD and AS children generally experience disruption in motor development and have lower muscle tone than others their age. Their poor muscle tone may be the source of their clumsiness, poor balance, and coordination problems, and difficulty manipulating small objects or tasks (i.e., tying shoes, threading beads, handwork such as crochet, etc.).

Visual-spatial processing helps you make choices about where or how to move, or how close to or far away from an object you should be. NLD and AS children experience deficits in this ability that clearly contribute to their sense of being "lost in space." The NLD or AS child actually gets "lost," at times even between one part of their school and another. The fact that most of us rely on visual information to remember directions should help us understand the significance of these deficits. Malls, bus stations, doctors' offices, and parks can be very intimidating if you can't remember your way from one place to another.

Dysgraphia

Dysgraphia, the inability to write, is a common characteristic of NLD and AS. For some students, this disability will be the only obvious discrepancy in their academic functioning and may be the reason they qualify for special education services. The problem is less an issue when these children are allowed to use a computer of some sort, yet there often remains significant difficulty committing ideas to written words—keyboard or not. This difficulty appears to involve a deficit in executive function, which we'll discuss later.

Motor Skills

Most of these children experience difficulty moving smoothly through the world: they often bump into things, jostle others in a hallway, and generally have trouble perceiving the boundaries around their own bodies. They drop things, bump, or spill more than other children, and it would follow that the experience of repeated failures and embarrassments adds to their anxiety, increasing the likelihood of another mishap.

It is important to recognize these problems early and to not resign the child to a life of poor coordination and few motor activities. Practice and structured instruction, even for things other children may find natural, is likely to be required. Riding a bike, tying a shoe, writing letters and sentences, being able to use public transportation—are all very necessary parts of an independent life. Finding a balance struggling to master a difficult skill that doesn't come naturally and developing compensation techniques is an important goal to strive for. For some individuals, repeated practice will be needed, along with a measure of maturity and the willingness to persevere in the face of frustration.

Sensory Integration

Sensory integration is the ability to organize the sensations of our day-to-day life. It is a neurological function, occurring at the brain level, usually without our thinking about it. Normally, our brain receives messages from many sources of sensory experience—what we see, smell, feel, taste, and hear from the environment around us. At the same time, we have internal messages being sent: how hungry we are, how hot or cold, what our muscles are doing, where our body is in relation to other people or objects, and information about our other body functions. Our brain integrates these messages—it organizes and prioritizes them. At least, that is what is supposed to happen.

When our ability to integrate sensory information goes wrong, our ability to interact with our environment is disrupted. For example, a child with sensory-motor problems may have trouble walking up or down stairs. Such a child will often use the railing for support, or walk one step at a time to maintain balance.

The human body uses three fundamental sensory systems: tactile, vestibular, and proprioceptive. The *tactile system* provides us with information about the texture, size, shape, and function of an object. Among many other things, it allows us to determine whether a touch is threatening or nonthreatening.

The *vestibular system* provides information through our inner ear about gravity and balance and about the position of our head and body in relation to the ground—in essence, information about whether we are standing, sitting, walking, or lying down, and about whether we can maintain balance in those positions. The *proprioceptive system* provides information through our joints and muscles about where the various parts of our bodies are and what they are doing. We all need these three sensory systems to function well and in concert with each other in order to function well ourselves.

Sensitivity to Sound, Touch, and Visual Stimuli

A common problem for children with NLD and Asperger's is sensitivity to sound, to touch, and to visual stimuli. Ranging from severe to mild in intensity, this problem can create significant disruption in everyday functioning. For many NLD and Asperger's children, hearing people talking in a classroom is so annoying as to be painful; touch that is intended as nonthreatening (a hug, for example) can be experienced as threatening; and colorful and exciting visual stimuli can be overwhelming and distracting. These responses to sensory information can interfere with their learning and can create behavior responses that add to the child's sense of not fitting in.

Isabella's Story

Isabella is a middle school girl with NLD who has significant sensory integration problems. While she is sitting in class, every sound other students make seems amplified times ten, and the sounds of everyday classroom life—the clock ticking and the sound of the pencil sharpener—all feel grating and annoying. As the day progresses, and she tries to block these sounds out of her mind, she becomes more irritable and more distracted. One day, she yelled at a classmate who was chewing gum, "JUST STOP THAT!" Isabella was asked to leave the class. She felt humiliated and angry; furthermore, she hadn't focused on any of the lesson that day, and she was falling further and further behind academically.

Arousal States

Children and teens with NLD and Asperger's syndrome have difficulty maintaining a constant or balanced level of arousal. *Arousal* refers to attention and concentration, and a general sense that the sensory systems of the body are working together. Optimal arousal is neither too high (overstimulated, hyper, agitated) nor too low (drowsy, distracted, no information going in). With NLD and Asperger's syndrome, children experience arousal states that are too high or too low, and as a result they experience attention, concentration, and behavioral problems that interfere with learning. There is an excellent program used in occupational therapy called the ALERT Program (Williams and Shellenberger 1994). This system (which we will not deal with here) is often helpful for NLD and Asperger's children.

In general:

- NLD and AS children are less likely to exhibit exploratory behaviors as toddlers; instead they use language to "explore." This reluctance to use motor activities and rely instead on language is often a lifelong tendency.

- NLD and AS children are late developing motor skills, such as learning to ride a bike, to play sports, or other gross motor activities.

- NLD and AS children often experience significant difficulty writing—the act of putting words to paper by hand.

Although many AS children are accomplished at art (not usually a favorite activity of the NLD child), creating the written word remains a problem for them as well.

- Low muscle tone tends to contribute to an odd, uneven somewhat hunched over manner of walking. Sitting at a desk, these children may also experience problems with posture.

- Attention and concentration are affected in NLD and Asperger's by changing sensory-motor input. The ALERT program is one that has been very useful for NLD and AS children.

Interventions for NLD and AS children will be discussed in part III of this book. Specific interventions for visual-spatial and sensory motor integration is best referred to an experienced occupational therapist, skilled in programs such as the ALERT program. Chapter 11 offers suggestions for developing a team to plan and provide services for your NLD or AS child.

6

Roots of the Matter: Information Processing and Organizational Problems

On any given day, each of us engages in a complex series of mental tasks just to get out the door in the morning. We automatically carry out our morning routines (grooming, dressing appropriately for the event and weather, and getting food and perhaps coffee). We often help other members of the family complete their routines, gather our supplies for the day, and carry out the motor activities that allow us to leave the house and get about our business. At times, this process goes more smoothly than at other times, but all in all we are able to multitask, that is, to carry on simultaneous activities with limited effort. In addition to this multitasking, we make many decisions about what to do, when to do it, and what is more or less important. Some of these decisions are small (sugar or no sugar in our coffee?), others larger (if I leave in ten minutes I might be late, should I delay or not?). Yet the process of carrying out all these activities, both mental and physical, occurs over and over each day.

Executive Function

Our morning routine is an example of a series of behaviors we have come to do more or less automatically. Throughout the day and throughout our lives, we establish many of these routines. They allow us to function on more than one level at a time (while fixing your coffee in the morning you can also review your day in your head and be prepared for what you need to do next). This ability is but part of an overall set of cognitive skills described as *executive function*. Executive function is a set of higher order, or more complicated, thinking skills that govern many different processes in our brain, such as language processes, cognitive processes, and motor processes. Executive function is thought to be under the control of the frontal lobe of the brain (see the illustration of the brain in chapter 1). In simple terms, executive function is the ability to:

- *Formulate* plans

- *Take action* on those plans

- *Delay action* when need be

- Operate on *multiple levels*

- *Integrate information* from one level to another. For example: while fixing coffee and thinking about the upcoming meetings that day, you realize you have little coffee left and add to your day a stop at the coffee shop for your favorite beans.

Routines and Rigid Thinking

For individuals with NLD and Asperger's syndrome, the executive function appears to be less than reliable. Although the establishment of routines is something most NLD and AS individuals find comfortable, they rigidly adhere to these routines. Most NLD and AS individuals have significant difficulty with multitasking and with integrating new information and taking appropriate action on it. Often, in day-to-day life, we rely on flexibility and spontaneity to successfully interact with others, varying our routines as needed to fit the situation. The ability to shift thinking, to read the situation and plan accordingly, is significantly disrupted in NLD and AS individuals. In essence, these children rely on a series of learned responses; they do not easily generalize from one situation to another. They seem to carry around an ever-increasing collection of internal scripts that help them order their world and let them know how to respond. In some ways, it is as if they have to translate the information in the world into a code or language they understand before they can respond with appropriate or predictable responses. This is not a very efficient system, and as the demands of day-to-day life become more complicated, the potential for error and problems increases.

Information Storage: The Dresser Drawers

The NLD or AS child's impairment in executive function affects planning, judgment, and overall social fluidity, but it also affects the child's ability to organize and integrate information for learning. For learning to occur, three things must be in place: attention, memory, and executive function. Learning requires that ideas and bits of information be assigned a category in the brain. It's sort of like putting away your clothes into your dresser drawers; it's easy to find what you need when all the T-shirts are in one drawer and the underwear in another. (Unless you're my son, but that's another story.) These categories store information at two levels: short-term memory and long-term memory. While we're learning new information, the area where attention and memory overlap is called the *working memory*. Only a certain amount of information can be stored in working memory; this is also a relatively short-term area, and information can be lost easily. Problems with planning and sequencing (executive function deficits) limit the usefulness of working memory, as irrelevant information may take up space in this storage area, sequences be lost, and important information not make it to long-term memory.

Slow Processing Speed

In a dresser, each drawer contains specific things decided upon by the owner. Yet throughout the process of learning, a concept or fact may have *many* categories it could fit into. The most effective system of organizing concepts or facts allows easy recall while at the same time making connections between related ideas. Without such an internal organization system (a dresser that has clothing in logical places) it will take longer to find information, and confusion easily sets in. This may be part of the reason NLD and Asperger's children suffer *slow processing speed*—it takes longer for these children to work problems, respond to directions, or complete activities. Their need for more time is difficult for teachers and parents to deal with, as the child seems to be *choosing* to move in slow motion. Nothing could be further from the truth, as the NLD or AS child feels increasing internal pressure to move quickly, yet cannot find the information he or she needs to know what to do next.

The unreliable and disorganized information storage system these children function with makes their working memory less helpful to them and thus makes the transfer of information to long-term memory inconsistent. Take for example learning about German shepherds. The primary category for organizing information about

German shepherds might be under the category "dog." While this is true—German shepherds are in fact dogs—it is a limited way to categorize or think about a German shepherd (shepherds have many unique and specific attributes, including a history of public service, and they are very different from pugs, which are also "dogs").

Creating these limited and rigid sets of thinking limits these children's capacity for integrative thinking—the ability to create meaningful links between information bits. This problem is often first noticed around the third grade, when the curriculum begins to demand the ability to organize and integrate information from multiple sources, rather than just reciting and remembering rote information. Activities such as writing a report or an essay usually give NLD and AS children difficulty, as their deficits in executive function and their other learning problems come to the foreground. The process of planning, ordering information, and, most critically, carrying out a project from start to finish becomes an almost impossible task for these children.

Metaphor, Analogy, and Humor

Without direct intervention, these children experience significant difficulty understanding metaphor and analogy. To understand metaphor or analogy is to understand how one thing stands for another—seeing the links between ideas. This skill seems to develop naturally. It is more highly developed in some people, but it is not usually the result of direct instruction.

It appears that somewhere along the path, NLD and AS children have missed developing this skill. They love words and use them without hesitation, yet analogy and metaphor do not come easily for these children. The cognitive rigidity mentioned earlier and these children's tendency to focus on the wrong detail make it easy to see why analogy or metaphor may be difficult for the NLD or AS individual to process. Understanding and participating in humor may have related causes. As mentioned in chapter 4, many NLD and Asperger's children and teens have trouble understanding and appropriately participating in the humor of their peers. This inability to joke along with peers only adds to their social isolation and sense of not fitting in.

Homework and Other Classroom Challenges

The NLD and AS child's problems of organization play out in obvious ways in their scholastic lives. These children rarely keep organized binders, nor do they get their assignments written down consistently. Papers and homework are lost, and reports and projects are disorganized jumbles of information that are rarely completed without significant parental intervention and many tears. Their deficits in executive function create real and persistent problems in their ability to create a personal organization system. As the demands of school increase with each grade, the NLD or AS child becomes a teen who is failing and who is unable to benefit from the traditional academic environment. Note-taking while listening to a lecture—multitasking at its best—is close to impossible for these students. Specific interventions are required if they are to succeed in the academic arena. Anger and punishment are unlikely to create positive results, but neither is reducing our expectations of these children the answer.

Focus on the Wrong Detail

NLD and AS children tend to focus on specific details and organize those details within rigid and limited categories. In the German shepherd example, an NLD or AS child may focus only the fact that the German shepherd is a dog. Yet if the teacher is presenting a story about World War II and the development of alternative methods of search and rescue (the use of these dogs being but one such method), the NLD or AS child may miss the point entirely and remember the story as being about a dog. Focusing on the wrong detail creates significant problems in comprehension for these children—problems that can baffle their teachers, who see children with high vocabulary and reading levels who don't seem to understand what they are reading.

Focusing on the wrong detail affects the NLD or AS child's ability to read between the lines, a skill most of us acquired without any direct teaching. If you are focused on the wrong detail of a lesson or social situation, you miss the nuances of meaning. You also are likely to misunderstand the action or response required from you. Their difficulties understanding cause and effect and anticipating the consequences of their actions can make NLD and AS children appear to teachers or peers as though they are deliberately violating rules or social norms. This is not the case, but without intervention, the NLD or AS individual has no way to even explain what the problem is—once again it as if they are speaking a different language than everyone else.

Novel Situations

These children's organizational problems and the rigid thinking also affect their ability to adapt to novel situations. Whether it is a result of frontal lobe dysfunction (as mentioned in chapter 1) or failure to develop an adequate theory of mind (as discussed in chapter 4), NLD and AS individuals have significant difficulty calling on past experiences and integrating that information with new circumstances to form a new plan of action. They are more likely to repeat a routine they know, almost as if they are following a script. When the old script doesn't work, or when there is no script for the situation, the NLD or Asperger's child or teen may experience a shutdown of sorts. This is very likely to occur when they encounter a situation that is overwhelmingly confusing and new.

Emotional Shutdowns and Behavior Problems

These shutdowns are often the source of the behavior problems, few as they may be, that are associated with NLD and AS—tantrums, refusal to work, or avoidance behaviors, such as leaving the room, putting the head down on the desk, or becoming "tired" and wanting to sleep. The NLD or AS child has no way to cope with a new situation that his or her existing mental routines cannot organize. When it's clear they are reacting to novel or confusing situations, these children's behavior should not be considered defiant or oppositional. This is not to say that their behavior problems should be accepted or encouraged, nor is it to suggest that the NLD or AS child should be protected from novel or potentially complex situations. Instead, a learning plan with many opportunities for the child to increase flexibility and add to his or her repertoire of experiences is essential. This approach, which will be discussed later in the book, helps the child develop a greater fund of information and lessens the likelihood that new situations will be seen as overwhelming.

Information Processing Deficit

As mentioned earlier, it is in many ways unfortunate the name nonverbal learning disability has been attached to this group of children. As we have come to see, the effects of both NLD and Asperger's appear more as a core deficit in information processing than one of "learning," per se. The disruption in these individuals' organization and planning skills is far-reaching and touches both social interaction and academic learning (see appendix E). The effects of these deficits include:

- Difficulties in planning, organizing, and integration of thinking

- Difficulties taking action and following through with problem solving in both academic and social settings

- Academic difficulties: homework is often lost or never even understood; schoolwork is incomplete or disorganized, and is experienced as overwhelming

- Dysgraphia (inability to produce written words) means taking notes during a lecture is extremely difficult; this often limits access to advanced courses

- Rigid, idiosyncratic thinking and slow processing time affect every aspect of functioning

- Poor adaptation to novel situations leads to poor social and academic functioning, emotional shutdowns, and behavior problems

- Difficulties with metaphor, analogy, and humor and failure to read between the lines cause poor comprehension and social alienation

- Difficulty anticipating consequences and accurately understanding cause and effect makes the world a frightening and random-seeming place

The effect of deficits in information processing underlies all areas of difficulty for the NLD or AS child, not just organization and academic learning. Social skills, pragmatic language, even sensory-motor integration are affected by information processing. Children with NLD and AS are likely to experience difficulties in any or all of the areas listed in appendix E. Program planning that includes interventions designed to take these deficits into consideration will be central to the success of these children.

Part III

Now What? Intervention and Program Planning

7

"Getting It": Addressing Deficits in Organizational Skills and Information Processing

In earlier chapters, we described how AS and NLD children's problems in social skills and visual-spatial and sensory integration and their specific learning deficits all result, to some degree, from a disorder of information processing. These children are likely to have above average intelligence, but the ways in which information goes into the brain, is stored in the brain, and is eventually used are all "off." In this chapter, we'll explore how the idea that NLD and, to some degree, Asperger's syndrome, are primarily disorders of information processing is helpful when we think about interventions and planning effective programs for these children.

It is very important that the families of NLD and Asperger's children understand and accept that this family member will need accommodations from the family for many years. Families with NLD and Asperger's children are forever changed by these children. These changes can bring great joy along with the inconvenience and hard work.

Information Processing Disorder

Ari's story in chapter 2 illustrated how an information processing disorder can interfere with a bright child's ability to do her schoolwork. Although clearly able to take in information, Ari was unable, even with the help of her mother, to produce the report on Native American housing assigned by her teacher.

The frustration experienced by both Ari and her mother is not unique. NLD and AS children and their families often encounter the pain of feeling unable to do what others seem to do easily, such as organizing separate pieces of information into a whole, cohesive project, idea, or paper. The mention of upcoming "projects" is enough to make parents of NLD and Asperger's children cringe. The assignment all too often becomes one for the parent, as the NLD or Asperger's child struggles to carry out tasks that may appear simple, but are to the child mysterious and confusing.

Problems of Organization

It's difficult for these children to maintain the organization of their schoolwork, home responsibilities, and basic day-to-day personal activities. Most NLD and Asperger's children do not readily adopt the organization methods presented in traditional classrooms, which typically rely on visual information such as the use of a binder with a list of daily assignments copied from the board. Organizing the binder itself, getting the homework done and back to school, and completing notes or sign-ups on time—all are organizational expectations that the NLD or Asperger's student cannot meet without direct intervention. The problem, as we have seen, is twofold:

1. The information is *processed* in an inconsistent manner and *stored* in memory in unusual and less than helpful ways.

2. The manner of *retrieving information* is poorly structured, and the child has to work extra hard to make the connections. This difficulty in retrieving information often results in frustration, and the child must extend extra effort just to maintain the will to continue to work.

Dealing with Novel Information

The NLD or AS child or teen can perceive practically all social situations and most academic experiences as "novel." These children have a limited ability to call upon previous experiences to help them in the current situation, and they won't process new information quickly enough to compensate for their lack of recall. But there are ways parents and teachers can help an NLD or AS child effectively deal with this deficit in his or her daily life; some concrete strategies are discussed in the paragraphs that follow.

Maintaining Routines and Setting Schedules

To reduce the child's sense that the world is novel, his or her daily routines should be consistent, clearly stated, and, when possible, posted on the refrigerator or some other central place. For children who don't read, parents can make a *picture schedule*. This is a series of pictures that either shows the child (or another child) doing an activity or is a symbol of the activity. The pictures can be drawings, photographs, or cuttings from magazines: for example, a drawing of a chair to remind the child to sit in the chair. At school, this series of pictures can be taped to the child's desk or to the inside of a binder or flipbook that the child carries. Another option is to post a picture schedule for the whole class on a bulletin board that is accessible to all students and thus more normalizing for the class. (The child may need to carry an additional picture or word schedule, as he or she will be likely to forget to look at the posted schedule.)

The schedule posted at home allows for the same predictability, even if there are changes for specific days of the week. The family of an NLD or AS child needs to maintain a consistent and predictable schedule, and the idea that less is more prevails. Scheduling activities for these children is necessary, but overscheduling or including the NLD or Asperger's child in the schedules or activities of other family members is difficult for the child and is often disruptive. For example, it would not be good idea to take the NLD or AS child to the soccer practice for a sister, then grocery shopping, then have the child sit for an hour and wait for the sister at ballet. It creates a hardship for many families to have to separate the schedules of the different children, and the concept may not fit well for families who prefer a "spontaneous" lifestyle or who have other pressing responsibilities. Yet without these accommodations, and without a willingness to adjust the family's activities, the NLD or AS child is likely to suffer. Creating a daily schedule at home may seem like a lot of work, but it is time that pays off in less confusion and resistance and fewer meltdowns during the day.

Ivan's Story

Ivan is in the first grade, and although he can read many words, his comprehension of what he has read is not strong. So although he can read instructions, he cannot necessarily follow them. The following schedule was designed by his behaviorist for use at school; a separate one was designed for use at home.

Ivan's schedule is written on two series of five- by eight-inch index cards; white for school and yellow for home. There is one card for each activity or time period Ivan needs to keep track of, and Ivan has the cards with him at all times in a handy and appealing Pokemon decorated cover. The group of cards is ordered according to his day and is held together by a ring clasp. The order can be changed, activities can be added or subtracted, and new cards can be made to help prepare him for changes. To add or subtract a card, Ivan's teacher or parent would explain the change and make sure Ivan saw it and understood. Ivan would likely ask about this change many times during the day.

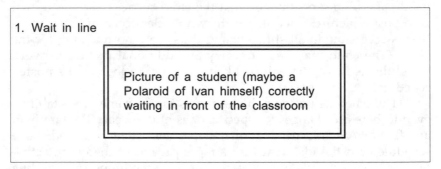

1. Wait in line

Picture of a student (maybe a Polaroid of Ivan himself) correctly waiting in front of the classroom

Figure 7.1   Ivan's School Schedule: A Sample Card

The list of possible cards for Ivan is presented below; each would have a picture or picture symbol and a phrase, similar to the example in figure 7.1. Explicit directions may be required for more unstructured time, such as recess or lunch. NLD and Asperger's students will have more problems during times of social chaos and unpredictable interactions with peers than in a classroom with a teacher and structured tasks.

1. Wait in line

2. Put lunch and coat away

3. Go to desk

4. Reading

5. Math

6. Put books away

7. Wait for recess

8. Recess (this may require more than one card)

9. Wait in line (copy of first card: the behavior is the same, make the card the same)

10. Music area

11. Story area

12. Lunch (many cards are possible here)

13. Wait in line

14. Go to desk (copy of card number three)

15. Art or spelling (two cards, used on separate days)

16. Pack up books

17. Check desk

18. Wait for dismissal

For home, the concept is the same. Ivan had the following list for after school, the development of which includes his parents and his psychologist.

---

1. Sit in the car with seat belt on

> Picture of a child, maybe Ivan himself, with a seat belt on

---

Figure 7.2 Ivan's Home Schedule: A Sample Card

1. Sit in car with seat belt on (Ivan does not like to do this)

2. Put coat and backpack in room

3. Wash hands

4. Snack in kitchen

5. Homework for 30 minutes

6. Computer time for 30 minutes

7. Set table with sister

8. Dinner

9. Bath

10. Brush teeth

11. Reading with Mom or Dad

12. Lights out at 8:30 P.M. and time for sleep

Preorganizational Skills

If a schedule is to be an effective tool, the NLD or AS child will need two sets of *pre-organizational skills*, or the skills that are needed if a person is to benefit from organization techniques. It is very important that parents and teachers begin to train the child in these skills at an early age and in differing ways for different settings (home, school, and community). The child will also need to practice them often. These skills revolve around a general ability to follow a set of expectations. These expectations could be a schedule, a direction to follow, or general social or behavioral guidelines. All of us follow rules or have expectations placed on us we need to meet. Learning to handle these expectations or follow the rules presented are valuable skills all children will need. Children should eventually master the following two skills:

- Looking for or knowing where to find the schedule (or the directions or the expectations). Although this may sound simple and obvious, the child will have to be reminded to look on the board for the schedule of the day, and he or she will have to practice, looking for it over and over, until he or she looks automatically. As these children mature, skills like knowing to look for the phone number to the Department of Motor Vehicles in the phone book under the State Government section will have to be taught and practiced.

- Following the schedule (or directions or expectations). These children will need practice following a schedule. They will need to be taught to check off the steps as they go, and to complete one thing before they start another.

Starting early is wise because both NLD and Asperger's students will need both of these skills in upper grades. It is also much harder to get into the habit of following a schedule if you start later. Specific techniques for learning to follow a schedule will need to be developed for these children in many different settings: at home, at school, and in the community.

Stress in Novel Situations

NLD and Asperger's children experience stress in *novel situations*— situations where they cannot predict what will happen next. Given that they rarely can predict what will happen in any but practiced situations, this experience of stress is frequent. Imagine what it would be like to experience day-to-day interactions and everyday expectations as new. Remember learning to ride a bike or drive, or the first day at a new school? These experiences are novel to most people the first time they engage in them. Remember the anxiety, the high level of attention required, and the uncertainty over what to do next? This experience is a common one for NLD or AS children, as they find most experiences novel.

Classroom Setup

As a way to reduce the stress, especially for younger children, a classroom for NLD or Asperger's students should be organized in a clear and uncluttered manner. Ideally, a work area should be designated, and should be separate from a reading area and from any other area the class might have, such as spaces for science, play, or art. This way, the students have an added cue about what sort of thing is happening in each area—even if the activity itself will differ from day to day.

Setup at Home

At home, the same concept applies. These children need an area that is *just* for schoolwork, where supplies and materials can be stored. This does not have to be a separate room; it can be a desk with a set of stacking shelves or baskets set aside for paper, folders, and schoolbooks. There should be limited distractions nearby; for example, the space should not be in front of a window, which can be very distracting. There should also be easy access to adults; in other words, the child should not be off in an area where no one checks on him or her and makes sure he or she is on task and getting work done.

As an adult, it is important that you model the behavior you wish the child to emulate. In plain terms, this means that parents of

NLD and Asperger's children need to organize their own lives as well as keeping the home environment and the life of the child organized. Although this recommendation may be difficult for adults dealing with the NLD or AS child, a good organizational structure must be modeled and supported in the home environment if you have any hope of creating fundamental change for the child. Some parents may need to hire a coach to help them meet the demands of organizing themselves. Life coaches who specialize in organizational skills can be an affordable and valuable resource for parents, and they are more and more available.

Slow Processing Speed

Slow processing speed involves the inability to quickly call up information in order to form an answer or a behavioral response. As we have discussed, it is an aspect of the information processing deficit these children exhibit. NLD and Asperger's children suffer for their slow processing speed in many situations—academic, social, and job-related—and throughout life, they will have to work to overcome this deficit. Though slow processing speed is clearly a problem at the brain level, to a certain degree this problem can be effectively dealt with. Three major interventions are of use in helping an NLD or AS child: openly discussing the issue; teaching focusing techniques; and teaching organizing techniques.

Discussing the Issue

As the child matures, *openly discuss* what the problem is. This intervention is central to all other interventions in this book. Give these children the language and the knowledge to understand what is happening to them. By no means does this mean you are granting the child permission to just accept the problem and not work to change. On the contrary, NLD and Asperger's children are empowered when they understand that they have strengths and weaknesses. Open discussion of their assets and deficits helps you support your child's strengths and help him or her take control of his or her weaknesses.

Teaching Focusing Techniques

For many of these children, their internal world interferes with their ability to focus on the activity at hand and is part of the processing speed problem. Clearing the clutter from their thinking (like clearing the clutter from their binders, their rooms, and their computers) is essential to many interventions that improve their organizational skills and information processing.

Learning to maintain focus allows the NLD or AS child to address the issue of slow processing speed as an ongoing and often-experienced problem. Maintaining appropriate focus will take practice. Often, the first issue in learning to focus is learning to ignore or deal with novel situations, which increase stress. Stress creates an internal interference with the child's input and retrieval of information—it's almost like a distracting noise.

Petunia's Story

Petunia is fifteen years old and has been riding public transportation for over a year now, having been taught by her mother how to get from home to her computer class on Saturdays. Things went very well until one particular Saturday when the bus was late and she missed her transfer at the next stop. Although she and her mother had rehearsed what to do if this situation came up, it also happened that an altercation between two other people occurred while she was waiting. She became overwhelmed by the noise and shouting and got up to move away from the problem. As she was walking away, a bus came, and Petunia found herself confused over whether this was a bus she could take or not. The more she thought about it, the more confused she became, and she forgot to do what she had been taught: get on the bus and *ask* if it was going where she wanted to go. Instead she sat immobilized for over twenty minutes until she calmed down enough to call her mother and get instructions about what to do.

Petunia has many skills, and she eventually dealt with the situation, though her NLD clearly affected her functioning. Her mother had done the right thing by teaching her several ways to solve problems: ask for information, sit and calm down, call home. This teaching evolved over many years, and Petunia is still likely to experience stress in unexpected situations throughout her life. Her best tool is the knowledge that she can get help and solve the problem.

Prewarning

Engaging in an interaction or being asked to meet an expectation, even in a familiar environment, can constitute a stressful novel situation. Whenever possible, the child should be *prepared* for the fact that new information is forthcoming, especially if that information will require a prompt answer. This technique is called *prewarning*, and it can sound like this: "I want you to clear your mind and focus on what I am about to say. I am going to ask you a question I need an answer to. . . ." This approach is also helpful if you want the child to perform a task, read out loud, or engage in an activity with others: "I will have Joan read, then Bobby, and then you, Sally. I will tap you on the shoulder to let you know your turn is coming. Everyone keep track of the reading as we go." Telling NLD and Asperger's children what is about to happen is central to their success at meeting expectations. Telling them you will ask them to repeat back what you said also increases their immediate attention. Not only does preparing the child for what is to come reduce the stress from novel situations (the situation or activity is now more predictable), but it helps the child clear his or her mind of any internal distraction that may be occurring.

Using physical proximity as part of the prewarning process can help—moving closer to the child, placing a hand on his or her shoulder (if the child can tolerate touch). Other physical cues can also help the child stay focused: a hand signal, an object placed on the desk, a verbal reminder (this should be agreed upon beforehand between student and teacher).

Teaching Organization Techniques

For many parents, it becomes second nature to organize their children. Many parents will say that, frankly, it's just easier to do it themselves. A word of caution is in order here. Teaching organization skills through doing the organizing *for* the child has a place in the continuum of learning, but only as a form of modeling and a means of supporting the child in acquiring new skills. To continue to organize these children—to clean their rooms, keep their binders in order, write their assignments down and check them off—in short, to take on the actual work of their organizational skills—can become a roadblock to their learning to do these things themselves. Strive to move from doing things *for* the child to doing things *with* the child to allowing the child to do things alone—and fail if need be. Failure helps these children (and all of us) develop coping skills and a tolerance for frustration. By high school, NLD and Asperger's children need to have some strategies they themselves understand for dealing with their disorder and the resulting organizational difficulties—unless, of course, their parents want them to remain at home with them forever, unable to function independently.

Computers and Technology

Teaching organizational skills requires consistency, simple and clear expectations, and a realization that this is a complex problem that will need to be addressed in all aspects of the child's life. The use of technology is a great asset, and will be discussed in more depth later in this book. Consider technology a positive—something to be used and modeled to help these children address a disability that affects their functioning. But keep in mind that although many NLD and Asperger's children will report that they have excellent skills on a computer, for many of them their computers are in fact as disorganized as their own brains. Learning good organization skills on the computer—using the file saving systems, folder hierarchies, and various data management programs—can teach them ways of organizing their own thinking that they might not otherwise understand. The computer becomes a wonderful analogy of their own minds.

Coding Systems

Systems of color-coding (using colors to denote various classes, chores, or other things that need to be organized) is often only of limited success. Color is not necessarily a key aspect of interest for many NLD children and therefore may not help them remember. Asperger's children may respond better to an organizational system that uses color. For example, a series of color folders or colored bindertabs, and a teacher who prints worksheets in the color to match, may help the child keep things where they belong.

A numbering system, an ordering system that uses words and numbers, or even a rhyming list that the child can remember can help. Various hand-held devices for making schedules and organizing information (especially the type that can feed information into a laptop or desktop computer) may become very useful for these children, especially as the technology improves.

Long-term Goals

Teaching organization is a complicated process, and frankly, no perfect system exists. Currently, the best systems that can be offered to these children are those designed and implemented by knowledgeable adults (parents and teachers alike) who are responsive to the challenges these children face. Programs are being developed, and as time goes by more effective models will likely evolve. Most NLD and Asperger's children will require organizational training and support for many years, and they will need adults who can consistently provide that support: a parent who operates as the child's case manager; a teacher with special training; an aide in the classroom.

It is essential that these children do not experience repeated failures at organization, and that they don't end up being punished for their disability. Creating adults who are dependent on others for their entire lives is not the goal of intervention with these children. The goal should be that, by the end of high school, NLD and Asperger's individuals are able to keep track of their own schedules, assignments, and commitments, and if they don't, that they are able to handle the consequences of this error. The goal is to help them develop techniques and use technology to remember and keep track of the information they need to function in the world.

Information Storage—Developing an Organizational Hierarchy

To learn, first we have to understand the information. Then we need some way of taking the information in and storing it in our memories for later use. An earlier chapter used the analogy of well-organized dresser drawers to illustrate how information is stored greatly affects the way we can retrieve it later. If underwear is sometimes put in the drawer with shirts and sometimes in the drawer with socks and sometimes alone in its own drawer, it will be very difficult to find it when we need some. The same is true for information. NLD and AS children need help putting their information away carefully, so we must design programs that help them develop a hierarchy of information—an organizational hierarchy.

Getting the Main Idea

Without realizing we were learning it, most of us learned how to understand the main idea of an assignment or a presentation—in other words, we "get it." We may argue about details, but we understand the main point. Not so for the NLD or AS child. These children miss the main idea, so they will not remember the purpose of a lesson, reading assignment, or lecture without help.

Helping the child learn to identify the main idea is one of the most useful interventions a teacher or parent can initiate. Learning to identify the key idea and then remember that idea will help the child learn to link ideas, finally finding the connections between items of information that elude him or her. Creative teachers develop practice activities for identifying the main idea. There are too many to describe here, and frankly, teaching the main idea is nothing new. What *is* new is getting across the need to do *more* of it for our NLD and AS students. This includes teaching and reviewing on this topic all the way through high school.

At home, parents can review with the child what the main point of a TV program or storybook was. Help the child keep the ideas simple and learn to sum up the main idea in one or two sentences. This is not a play-by-play retelling of the story. It is learning to see the forest and ignore the trees, as the saying goes.

For example, Kevin has watched his favorite Saturday morning cartoon with his brave father, who sat through it with him. At the end of the program, his dad asks him, "What do you think this program was about, Kevin?" Kevin may start to retell the show in no particular order, just hitting on the action scenes or whatever caught his eye. His dad, who had been paying attention (and maybe even keeping a few notes for himself, as these characters are new to him), helps Kevin review the main idea of the show. "Well, these things are true, Kevin. But let's see, the main idea of the show was how Bobby didn't follow directions and got lost and his friends had to rescue him." Notice how Kevin's dad lets Kevin try to tell him what the show was about and acknowledges that his observations are true. The father also uses the term "main idea" to reinforce that that's what he wants to hear.

This exercise opens up the possibility of discussing related ideas, uses language as a means of interacting, and teaches the concept of main idea in a fun way. A word of caution: keep the "teaching" to a sentence or two, like Kevin's dad did. Long-winded discourses on the point of the TV show will lose the child as easily as the show did. Be patient with your child (and yourself); this is actually a very difficult task.

To really achieve success teaching main idea, begin early and reinforce the concept often. Many teachers will tell parents they already do this. No doubt this is true, and the reinforcement provided is enough for the usual students. But for the NLD or AS student, the already-designed curriculum is unlikely to be enough, and extra focus and practice will be needed.

Metaphor, Analogy, and Reading Between the Lines

NLD and AS children are concrete thinkers; they take things as they are. To them, words mean one thing, and one thing only. Obviously, this does not reflect reality, especially in a language like English, where words and phrases commonly have more than one meaning. For example, the phrase "put the card in your hand" has different meanings based on the context. If you were at an event where you need to hand a card to someone, you would put the card in your hand and hold it out. But if you were playing a card game, this phrase would mean to add the card to the cards in your "hand," meaning the group of cards you already have.

The use of double meanings of language has been a source of humor probably as long as humans have been able to speak. NLD and AS children have real trouble understanding such forms of humor. This is not because they are stupid, as they often feel, but because the source of this humor is not something they understand easily. The ability to "read between the lines," the subtle skill of understanding implied meanings, is similar. These children do not understand subtle or implied meanings, and this can lead to social embarrassment.

Their reliance on concrete thinking and literal interpretation of language affects their understudying of analogy and metaphor. Analogy (drawing a comparison or pointing out a resemblance between different things) is used often in literature and even in everyday language. Teachers use analogy in lesson presentation all the time; for example, comparing the internal structures in a cell to an engine that powers the cell. In our culture, not understanding analogy makes for moments of confusion, and it is likely to affect learning.

Understanding metaphor creates similar problems. Metaphor is the use of language to describe one idea using another idea. Describing the organizational system of the brain as being a dresser with drawers for information storage is a metaphor. Many NLD or AS children would not find this image helpful without an explanation. That explanation would need to convey the idea that the dresser with drawers is just a way to think about the brain, a way to imagine in understandable words what the brain may be doing (storing information like you store clothes).

Throughout history parents have taught moral ideas using fables and parables, which convey ideas through metaphor. The stories of the boy who cried wolf and the tortoise and the hare, for example, teach us lessons about ourselves using metaphors. For the NLD or AS child, the point of these stories may be missed; the trees may become the focus, not the forest (and that saying itself is another example of the use of metaphor).

The child who cannot figure out metaphor and analogy will feel left out, not part of a group of people who understand these uses of language. For that reason alone it becomes important to teach directly what an analogy or a metaphor is, how to identify each and, when possible, how to understand them. For the NLD or AS individual, it may never be the case that use of metaphor or analogy comes naturally. That isn't necessary. All that is needed is that these children learn to understand and recognize this form of communication and, hopefully, to decipher and even appreciate it in literature, in the classroom, and in conversation.

The Devil Is in the Details

Focusing on details is important in learning. Details add color and spice to ideas and concepts in many fields of knowledge, and they help many of us remember information. Unfortunately, the NLD or AS child focuses on details that are often not those that are central to a concept, but are unusual or unrelated bits of information. An inability to find the main idea and a tendency to focus on the wrong details add to these children's problems with reading between the lines. This problem is clearly related to their overall information processing deficit. The child who listens to the story of Little Red Riding Hood and doesn't understand that the wolf has replaced Grandma and is trying to trick (and eat!) Red has missed the main idea. The child may have focused instead on the picnic lunch Red was carrying and begins to think about what would be in the lunch, what he or she likes for lunch, and maybe what's for lunch today. This line of thinking has taken the child far afield of the story and in a direction different from that taken by most of his or her classmates.

Focusing on the wrong detail will affect these children in many ways. Not only are they likely to miss a detail they need to know from an assignment, they often make mistakes in following the directions on a worksheet. When the class is following along reading from a textbook, the NLD or AS child may be on the wrong page, unaware what the problem is but feeling confused that he or she doesn't understand what is going on.

Designing Organizational Interventions

In all situations (on worksheets and tests, and in verbal directions at home, at school, or elsewhere), the best interventions follow these guidelines:

- Directions are simple and clear

- The fewer directions at a time, the better

For example, give one or two directions, wait for those to be followed, then give one or two more. Follow these concepts in all dealings with these children. Keep in mind their processing speed issues, and never assume they know what you mean. Telling an NLD or AS child, "I don't want to see you eating candy in my class again!" may only succeed in getting him or her to eat in class when you are not looking. The child's literal or concrete understanding of that statement can lead him or her to feel the emphasis is on *where* you see him or her eat. Eating when you're not looking is not an attempt to manipulate you or be a class clown.

Assuming the child knows how to do a task may actually interfere with the child's ability to follow the directions. For example, an AS student has a school chore to empty the classroom garbage cans and take the garbage to the large bin in back of the school. The teacher's assumption that he knew how to do this effectively was incorrect. He clearly could take out garbage—he did it at home. But at school, he transferred the skill from home *exactly*, that is, he took one bag at a time all the way to the back of the school to the large bin. This resulted in ten trips to the bin, taking him significantly longer than his teacher intended and making him late for his bus. It wasn't until his teacher discovered the problem and taught him to empty *all* the classroom bags into one large bag and then take that one to the bin, that he was able to solve the problem.

Stress Management and Effective Teaching

For learning to occur, not only must the teaching be effective, but students also need to have control of their stress. All the ideas and suggestions for interventions in this book will be less than useful if the child is overwhelmed by stress. As we have discussed in this chapter, effectively managing stress requires many levels of intervention at home and at school. No matter what the particular effects NLD or AS has on them, these individuals will almost constantly have to deal with some aspect of their disorder. In terms of stress management, time management, appropriate planning, effective action taking, and all the many other aspects of executive function, small successes may be all a parent experiences for many years. Yet it is important to hold these children accountable for their work and their responsibilities. The distinction between infantilizing the child by doing too much for him or her, and overwhelming the child by not providing support is a fine one. But parents need to find and hold that line at each developmental level, or the child they will never develop his or her true potential.

8

Learning to Learn:
Interventions for Successful
Learning Experiences

The development and use of organizational skills is one of the cognitive processes that are part of executive function. As we discussed in chapter 1, the executive function is our ability to plan and predict and to organize and use information. These skills are under the control of the frontal lobe, which oversees our thinking, judging, learning, and social skills. Individuals with highly developed executive function are good at planning and organization; they read social cues and adapt readily to novel situations. They display flexibility and adaptability in their lives. The opposite is true for people with NLD or Asperger's: rigid thinking and reliance on routines are usually the main ways these children survive. For people with these disorders, it is hard to learn the skill of flexibility. There is no prepackaged program to date designed specifically to reduce these children's rigidity and increase their flexibility in day-to-day situations. The best we can do is incorporate certain guidelines into program planning.

Using Planned Exposure

Exposure to increasingly different activities and experiences should be planned so it does not overwhelm the child. But planned exposure does not imply controlling the child's environment to such a degree that he or she has no life experiences to draw on and no practice at being flexible. For some children, carefully chosen outside activities—once-a-week clubs, camps, or activity classes—are a good way to start. These activities may be different than the child's accustomed school activities: for instance, there may be fewer accommodations or more demands. Take horseback riding, for example, which involves exposure to an animal, a new setting, and a new set of expectations and stimuli. Though animals are often perceived as unpredictable to the child, actually they are usually following a defined set of "behavior rules" specific to their species. This can make interaction with the horse rewarding for the NLD or Asperger's child who can learn these new rules: this activity taps into these children's sense of routine but also adds to their ability to adapt. (See appendix D for other activity ideas.)

Planning for Increased Social Expectations

As children mature, increasing the expectations placed on them means they'll need more teaching about how to handle life situations. Social pressures in middle school and high school are much more complex than those in elementary school, and activities with age-mates brings with it demands for more sophisticated social skills. Teaching these social skills requires careful planning and thought, but it is important to keep the child from becoming isolated as he or she matures. Activity clubs that tap into the child's special interest are a good way to include the child in a social setting with only limited unstructured time. A sport the child cannot do or a club that is full of "free time" to socialize would not be a good choice as these are not likely to be highly successful activities.

Allowing Ample Time

NLD and Asperger's children are smart enough to figure out what might be a good plan in many situations; they just can't do it quickly, and the situations usually don't afford them the time they need. In such cases it is important that the child has been taught coping strategies such as remaining calm, asking for help, or speaking up—for example, "I'm not too quick with words; give me a few minutes and I'll let you know." Many NLD and AS children and teens develop their own idiosyncratic ways of stalling and coping in stressful situations; few of these are usually functional in the long run.

Brian's Story

Brian has significant difficulty in thinking on his feet, and he is often in the situation of explaining what he is doing. This is partly because he is sixteen and partly because, with NLD, he has a relatively self-centered world view. He goes about doing whatever he thinks is right without thinking about all the implications of his actions. One morning, after arriving at school, he discovered he didn't have any pencils with him. To get all the credit for the day in his homeroom, students were required to arrive prepared—this included having the supplies they needed. Brian knew this requirement, and he chose to go into the classroom and rummage around on the teacher's desk looking for a pencil to "borrow." When the teacher found him going through her desk and confronted him gently, he stammered and stalled, "Well ... uh, uh ... I ... uh, uh ...," and never answered her. As he struggled for words, filling the space with meaningless chatter, she finally got angry with him. At this point he was too upset to explain himself at all. He would have explained what he was doing (even though it was a poor solution to his problem), but he relied on an old stalling technique he learned early in life. This technique rarely works for him: when he avoids answering a question, the other person either fills in the answer for him or becomes angry with him. In the situation with his teacher, if Brian had been able to take a breath he might have been able to focus on a simple rule: answer the question, and only the question, dealing with one idea at a time. He might have been able to start a dialogue in which he could explain his thinking, flawed though it may have been, and feel some sense of resolution with his teacher.

Predicting Outcomes

Practicing "What would happen next?" is often part of a good pragmatic language program with a speech therapist. This technique involves watching an acted scene or reading about an event without an ending and "predicting" what would happen next. The child or group discusses options and learns some general concepts about how behavior is likely to occur. Predicting outcomes is a very valuable skill organizationally, academically, and socially. It helps facilitate organization, scheduling, and developing a repertoire of behaviors. Without this ability, not only do children feel ill prepared for general functioning, they cannot react well to unpredictable events, nor do they learn from these experiences, as their anxiety prevents any learning from making it into meaningful memory.

New Coping Strategies

These children's reliance on rigid rules and routines is in fact a coping strategy. Life is unpredictable and confusing, and these routines and rules make the child feel safe. For many NLD and AS children, these routines develop into obsessions and compulsions, as discussed in chapter 3; in this case the child requires referral to individual and group therapy aimed at treating obsessive-compulsive disorder. This treatment can be an important ingredient in an overall program for the NLD or AS child. But removing these methods of coping without helping the child develop more effective techniques is likely to create a great deal of stress, as he or she is then defenseless against the stress and sense of confusion that are likely to follow. It is important to work with the child to establish healthy and effective coping strategies.

Maintaining Attention and Concentration

Almost every issue facing the NLD or Asperger's child is made up of overlapping problems, and because of that, overlapping interventions are needed. Processing speed is affected by attention and concentration, and attention and concentration are limited by these children's slow processing speed—as the brain processes the information more slowly or less effectively, they often lose attention, becoming distracted and going off-task. In some ways, it's a chicken-and-egg problem; does the problem with processing speed cause the attention problems or do the attention problems cause the slow processing? Problems with attention, concentration, and processing speed in turn affect a child's overall organizational skills.

Whatever the cause, maintaining attention is a problem for these children that requires direct intervention. Although medication may be recommended for difficulties of attention, recall that all NLD and Asperger's children with problems of attention do not suffer AD/HD (attention deficit disorder). Interventions that move beyond medication may be needed to address these issues, including the following:

- Remove distractions and clutter. As a general rule for NLD and Asperger's children, less is more—less paper, fewer instructions, less visual clutter, less noise. Clearing the clutter also refers to these children's need for clean and orderly workspaces. The workspace should be a specific area that is away from visual and auditory stimulation like Nintendo or

TV. Classrooms with busy, visually overwhelming decorations and displays are not the first choice for these students. The work area at home should follow the same concept.

- Provide headphones with music to help the child focus during work time. In general, NLD and AS children benefit from access to a portable stereo or a computer with headphones to use while they're working. They will be less likely to be distracted by the ticking clock or another student chewing gum or tapping a pencil and more likely to remain focused on their own work.

- Seat NLD and Asperger's children in the front of the classroom. As with other students with attention problems, this seating plan reduces these children's tendency to be distracted by other classroom events or other students.

- Let them move. NLD and Asperger's children are likely to need permission to get up from their seats periodically. Some access to movement can actually help these students maintain attention.

As you can see, the need for a classroom that accommodates these children's needs is a strong one. See appendix C for a "wish list" describing the ideal classroom for an NLD or AS student.

Time Management Problems

Problems with managing all aspects of time are common for the NLD or AS child and teen. These problems are many, and they affect both the child and the family. Some of the most prevalent issues these children have include:

- They are often late, as they don't keep good track of time.

- They tend to feel pressured by any time constraints.

- They misjudge time—how much is left, how long something will take, how long they or others have been talking.

Keeping Track of Time

The simple intervention, and one that is often overlooked, is teaching the child to tell time and use a watch. This may sound obvious, but NLD and AS children often have trouble learning to tell time and will need specific, patient, and repeated teaching on this topic. In our culture, there is a tendency to use digital clocks or watches: they display a number and the child can easily give the correct answer when asked what time it is. But there is no way to use the digital watch to teach the relative aspects of time; for example, how long it is from 10:30 to 10:45. On a digital watch this is just a series of numbers that appear on a screen. To help the NLD or Asperger's child understand time, use a clock or watch with hands. The movement of the minute hand and the second hand around the face of a clock or watch is a much better tool to teach about the passage of time than digital numbers flashing at the child. As we'll see in the next section, a watch with a timer will be useful for other interventions and is therefore preferable.

Learning to Notice Time

Using a watch to notice time is an example of learning to look for the solution to a situation and learning to follow a plan (or schedule or expectation). The first step to mastering time is to *notice* it. To teach noticing time, begin with two simple time assignments each of which deals with a separate aspect of time. One type of assignment involves activities you want the child to do *at a certain time*, such as, "Your assignment today is to tell me when it is 5:00 P.M." or, "Your job in class is to signal when it is time to switch to computer lab." A watch with a timer or alarm is often useful and helps remind the child to look at the watch.

A second type of assignment involves activities you want the child to do for a *certain amount of time*. Using a timer, preferably one with a large area that shows time passing in a separate color, is helpful. Practice having the child do things for shorter or longer time periods. Ask him or her to compare the differences in time by having them experience activities of differing time periods. For example, cooking may be a good activity to use (food is a good motivator), or perhaps a stretching activity wherein the child holds a stretch for differing lengths of time (this has many benefits, but is unlikely to be popular). Asking these children to estimate how long they have been riding or eating dinner or watching a TV show is a good way to help them internalize the sense of time passing. An hourglass with sand is another great visual for this concept.

Planning and Taking Action

Executive function deficits affect the NLD or AS child's ability to plan and follow through with those plans. Add to that the child's problems with time management and the result is problems planning workloads or balancing activities and responsibilities. Many an NLD or AS child has been known to make errors in judging the length of time it will take to complete an assignment or activity. Being chronically late to class may be partly a result of these children's being "lost in space" and losing track of where they are, but it also may be due to their having no concept of how long it takes to get from one room to another and how long it takes to pack up a backpack. These children are not trying to avoid class, and they're not having fun by missing the start of a class—the opposite is more likely true, as entering a class late is embarrassing.

Even after weeks have gone by, the child will likely continue being late without clear, focused teaching about what is wrong (time management) and how to fix it (a plan for packing a backpack and getting to class, complete with the route). Just telling the child he or she is in the wrong by being late will not fix the problem, and assuming it will indicates a lack of understanding of NLD and AS. For change to occur, the child will need a plan to address the problem. The plan will need to take into account what the problem is with getting to class (it could be many things). Then it will need to detail what the child needs to do to avoid the problem or to fix it. Finally, the plan will need to be practiced repeatedly before any hope for change can be expected.

The best solution for classwork and other assignments is for the child to get assignments ahead and for the parents to help the child plan the week or month. Daily assignments are most difficult, and they shouldn't be given to the NLD or Asperger's student until high school. It will take practice and planning for these children to get their time management skills under enough control to handle six different classes with daily assignments in each. For some, this may never happen and a different schedule will be required—block scheduling or classes coordinated to allow for limited homework assignments. (Block scheduling involves fewer, longer classes per day than a traditional schedule.) Clearly, these children will need support for many years.

Learning Modalities

Most of us have a preferred *learning modality*, that is, a way of taking in information that we find helps us remember the information better. The majority of people would describe themselves as "visual learners": people who remember what we *see* more than what we *hear*. In truth, all of us get information from what we see, hear, feel, and even smell all the time, and we hardly separate that information by source in our conscious thinking. But when it comes to what we remember the most, each of us has a modality of learning that works best.

The Auditory Modality

There are people who learn more effectively through the *auditory modality*; that is, when information is primarily presented through auditory channels—and NLD and AS children are among these learners. These learners benefit from oral presentation of material, oral practice and review, and even from assessment that is presented orally. This is not to say they do not benefit from other modalities. The *kinesthetic modality*, or learning through body and motor activities, and the *visual modality*, or using what is seen to remember information, are also great contributors to their learning. Activities such as labs or skits, are wonderful learning components, as these activities involve both visual and kinesthetic learning. Yet the majority of NLD and AS students will utilize auditory information as a primary source of learning. As mentioned earlier, they appear to have a relative strength in auditory memory and auditory processing, and they tend to rely on this information over other channels of learning, such as visual or kinesthetic.

Other Learning Style Considerations

In addition to occurring through perceptual modalities (visual, auditory, kinesthetic), learning also occurs either *sequentually* (step-by-step learning) or *simultaneously* (whole-concept learning). Just as each of us has a modality preference, each of us has a preferred style—though, again, most learners take in information both ways. Our preferred style impacts how we learn in various settings, which may or may not adhere to our needs.

An NLD or Asperger's child is most likely a *sequential learner*. The characteristics of these children's preferred learning style are as follows:

- Step-by-step learning. This includes simple numbered directions, with each step defined and each component explained in order.

- Logical explanations that include details. These children will *require* logical explanations.

- Information presented as fact and figures. Note that the NLD or AS child will not necessarily see the connections between these pieces of information.

As learners, NLD and AS children tend to:

- Be perfectionistic

- Learn to read and spell phonetically

- Memorize rules (for language, math, and other subjects)

- Not do well with inferential learning (see below) or problem-solving approaches to learning; they need guided and planned learning experiences.

- Need structured, predictable, routine, learning environments

- Be part-to-whole learners; that is, they learn the parts of a concept in order to learn the whole concept. In this respect the NLD or AS child is the opposite of a simultaneous learner, who learns the whole to learn the part.

Inferential learning is learning that the child figures out for himself or herself after a series of experiences or activities designed to illustrate a point, a rule or a concept. NLD and AS children are unlikely to succeed with this type of teaching. This is important for parents to know when they are considering kindergarten or preschool programs, as some programs are designed specifically with the inferental style of learning in mind. Such preschools are unstructured, offering learning experiences (instead of lessons) and requiring the child to "discover" concepts without recourse to a planned program. These are preschools that would not be helpful for the NLD or AS child.

Planning a Program around Learning Modality

It is important that parents and teachers understand the child's preferred learning modality and design a program that uses the child's learning strengths to support his or her educational progress. Even with a diagnosis of NLD or Asperger's, any individual child will not fit 100 percent with the picture presented here. A good assessment is essential, and classroom activities and materials should reflect the information about the child's learning style and needs that results from this assessment.

However, in general, most NLD and AS children will learn new information best if it is presented auditorily or in a modified lecture format, as follows:

- Use lecture format in conjunction with technology support to eliminate the need for multitasking, i.e., note-taking while listening (this technology will be discussed shortly)

- Present information in small segments with review and summary after each segment

- Intersperse the teaching monologue with attention-getting and review tools

- Use brief activities to make a point

- Use question and answer "moments" to keep the student involved and continually *summarizing* the information presented

- Use visual examples (pictures, video clips, Internet sites) and physical activities (skits, labs)—because no one learns in one modality alone

As a source of review and to help students get through more advanced or detailed material, books on tape are a great tool for NLD and Asperger's children, particularly for literature and history courses. These tapes can greatly add to the child's learning experience and increase his or her enjoyment of literature.

Textbooks and Worksheets

Often NLD and Asperger's students find worksheets and textbooks visually confusing. In the past few years, textbook makers and school districts have chosen to move in the direction of more and more visually complicated materials. For some students without NLD or Asperger's, the use of colors and pictures and separately boxed information is interesting, and is reported to actually help them learn. Not so for the NLD or AS student. In many cases, the teacher may need to redo worksheets: to copy them in black and white with the visually confusing areas covered over. Some worksheets just have too much on a page—a math sheet with thirty problems may be overwhelming to these children. Having that sheet copied with every other row covered over, so that the new sheet has more white space and is less visually confusing, may be a great help. Note that it is not enough to just tell the child to "do every other problem," as is common in some schools. The worksheet itself needs to be presented in a less visually overwhelming manner. As the student matures, it is a good idea to limit this practice and to help the child learn to accommodate to more visual clutter and a greater workload.

Multitasking

Multitasking as a concept is clearly a product of our current culture. The ability to do more than one thing at a time is often viewed as a strength, and in some jobs, it's a requirement. For NLD and AS students, multitasking is overwhelming. Single-tasking (a fancy way of saying "just doing one thing at a time") is often enough to ask of them as they struggle to follow through with plans and tasks one at a time. As they grow older, the single most glaring example of these children's inability to multitask is their inability to take notes while listening to a lecture. To succeed in higher education, this skill is a necessary one. Without learning to multitask in this manner or developing some modification that fulfils the same functions as lecture notes, these students are denied access to more advanced subject matter and learning experiences.

Technological and Other Modifications

Advances in technology can be of special help for NLD and AS students. Their problems in note-taking while listening to lectures can be addressed with the use of special whiteboards that allow the notes the teacher writes on the board to be directly downloaded onto the students' laptops. These whiteboards (sold under the name of Softboard, Webster, and Smartboard, to name a few) make it possible for the student to listen to and focus on the teacher while the notes the teacher is putting on the board appear on the screen of the laptop. When the student studies, he or she opens a file of the notes for that particular lecture and has the material to review. There is no way to directly inject the information into these students' brains, so they still have to study (see the study skills section later in this chapter), but the process of getting the information is clearer and more appropriate for their learning needs. This modification requires that:

1. The school has the Softboard (or similar whiteboard)

2. There is an appropriate computer for the teacher

3. The student has his or her own laptop

The whiteboard technology for classrooms is an investment that has the potential to serve many students. In the long run, this technology is more cost effective and more empowering for the students than having individual aides taking notes for each NLD or AS student. Aides taking notes is an often used modification that clearly has the advantage of personal contact, but its disadvantages are that the student can easily lose the notes and that the student is not in charge of his or her own learning but is dependent on another person. For some students, the aide is necessary for other reasons, primarily social and organizational, but for students aspiring to greater independence and to a future in the working world or higher academics, dependence on an aide is not ideal at the middle school or high school level.

A simpler modification is the use of a tape recorder. This is good for younger students, and it requires less technology. A small tape recorder carried by the child can be used to record lectures in classes and the child's *notes to self*. Notes to self are just what they sound like—messages the student or aide tapes to remind the student of things to do that day. In addition, the teacher can make tapes for the student and parents explaining assignments or reminding them of things the student is working on. The child usually appreciates the personal note that having the teacher's voice at home brings. Taped information can also be very helpful to confused parents who are trying, with varying levels of success, to understand their child's version of what the child needs to do. Speech therapists and clinical psychologists can also use tapes made for the child to reinforce skills the child is working on—relaxation skills, behavioral cues, and assignments for social interactions, to name a few.

Concept Formation and Problems in Learning

NLD and AS students find themselves learning large amounts of seemingly unrelated bits of information. Even on topics that interest them, their difficulties with organizational thinking and integrating of information make for a limited repertoire of generalizable concepts. Left to their own devices, these students tend to find themselves forever unable to move beyond a series of facts.

Personal Projects and Mentor Teaching

One of the most valuable learning experiences for NLD or AS students is the development of their skills at self-directed projects. The use of student defined projects as a central part of the learning experience is a focus of the program at the Orion Academy (as previously mentioned, Orion is a high school specializing in teaching NLD and Asperger's syndrome students). In a program called "personal projects," students work with a mentor teacher to plan, organize, and carry out an individual learning project that they present to the school community every six weeks. There are four different types of projects defined at Orion: exploratory, breadth, depth, and personal growth. Students must produce work in each area during the year. The school has defined a program that includes producing weekly logs, developing outlines, and learning information gathering. The final step, producing a presentation, is as important as learning the information itself—as the students learn, if you can't explain what you have learned to another person, the fact that you know it may be of little use to you. In addition, the presentation requirement addresses the need to help these students keep in mind their audience; they must focus on the perspective of another person.

The fact that the *process* of carrying out the project is more important than the *content* of the project creates an exciting learning environment for the students. Furthermore, it's one where parents are not responsible for the work their children produce. To understand how to find information on a topic of personal interest, how to gather that information in an effective manner, and, most importantly, how to organize that information into a meaningful whole that others can benefit from, is to have learned how to learn. When NLD and Asperger's students succeed in this endeavor, they are making progress in an activity that can keep them learning throughout their lives.

Pattern Learning

A problem seen in both NLD and AS students is their overreliance on learning patterns. This style of learning is often seen as a strength that the child relies on for skill development. Teachers and parents have used this strength to help the child develop success in playing sports, memorizing facts, and learning the routine for the day. Unfortunately, this strength brings problems when the child relies solely on the pattern without learning the concept or recognizing the overall point of an activity. Learning to serve a volleyball by practicing a pattern of motor skills may be very helpful for a child. But the fact that she has no idea about the overall point of serving the ball in the game of volleyball is a disadvantage for her. She is still not ready to play with others, as she is focused only on that part of the game—serving—that she has learned.

For another example, many NLD and AS students experience difficultly with math, especially fractions. Well-meaning teachers often teach these children the *pattern* of converting fractions to decimals to make adding, subtracting, multiplying, and dividing fractions easier. This method may be useful in the short run. There is less stress and the students get the right answers. Yet they have no idea what a fraction is; the concept still eludes them. When they get to algebra and are confronted with numbers presented in fraction format as part of equations, they don't know what to do. The pattern they learned gets in the way and has to be undone before learning can continue.

Study Skills and Homework

The organizational deficits these children have profoundly impact the areas of study skills and homework. Like students with other forms of executive function deficits, NLD and AS children experience difficulty successfully completing homework across the board. The problem arises not only in knowing what the homework is, but in getting the work and materials home, completing the work at home, and, once it's complete, successfully turning it back in to the teacher. In addition, when the homework is to "study," the NLD or Asperger's student is often unsure what "studying" entails and has real trouble following through.

Homework Support

Several interventions can help these students clear the organizational hurdles they face in getting their homework done and turned in:

- In general a second set of books should be kept at home. This eliminates the need for transporting them and makes for fewer things to be forgotten or lost.

- Homework should be assigned for the week, and special projects should be assigned as far ahead as possible. Projects should have review points throughout the process so that the entire project cannot be left to the last night.

- Homework should be listed on the Internet so student and parents can check to be sure it is all done. If that is not feasible, there should be a coordinated system set up between home and school. For example, a teacher will create a homework sheet for the student. The student writes down the work for each week, the teacher signs it to verify it's correct, and the parent initials it when the work written down is in fact completed at home. This system is useful in early grades to teach the child the skill of keeping track of homework and to give the parents a simple way to make sure it is followed up on.

- A laptop computer, if available, limits the amount of paper transferred from school to home and back—and potentially lost. Students can work on papers scanned into the computer and then either bring the work back to school in the computer itself or e-mail it to the teacher upon completion.

- For ongoing organizational issues, the use of a privately hired coach for the child is often helpful. These people are usually teachers who have developed a speciality in working with disorganized students. They work one-on-one with the child to develop organizational skills and liaise with the school to develop a plan to make these skills work for the child. Often what these children resist doing for a parent they will do for a coach, teacher, or other adult.

Study Skills

Study skills are valuable, and need to be taught directly and reinforced often. It is never too early for the child to start developing good study habits. The NLD or Asperger's student will need to have "studying" explained and taught, just like the other skills he or she needs to learn. Never assume that because the child tells you he or she is "studying" that the child has any idea what that means.

To study effectively, children need to learn to:

- Pay attention to charts and diagrams in their books. Teach them these as shortcuts to understanding and remembering key points.

- Define the main idea of an assignment. If they cannot find the main idea, teach them to ask for help, as this is the single most important way to improve their information retrieval and the development of organized thinking.

- List all vocabulary and key words in the reading or the chapter, then review them by being quizzed by a parent or classmate.

- Remember that when a reading assignment is made, the teacher will likely have a discussion of the material. Teach the child to take time to review the reading and predict some possible discussion topics that the teacher might ask about.

Here are some ways to foster good study skills:

1. **Plan a definite time for studying and stick to it.** There are different ideas about when study time should be. The argument for having the child study immediately after school, before any playtime, is based on experiences with students who find it difficult to give up a play or free-time activity. For these students, the shift back to a work or study mentality is too difficult and the result is a tantrum or poor work quality. However, some other children cannot regroup and

maintain the attention and concentration needed for homework without a break. The decision about when to schedule the homework time should be based on the style and needs of the child. The important point is to pick a time and stick to it, making studying and homework the *only* things that happen during this time.

2. **Divide study time into segments of no more than thirty minutes.** Arrange five- to ten-minute breaks between studying segments. For elementary school students with NLD or Asperger's, studying an hour a night is plenty. By middle school, the student should be working toward increasing this to one and a half hours every few days, and by high school the student should be able to tolerate two hours of studying (with breaks, the study period as a whole lasts about two and a half hours). Keep in mind that the slow processing speed experienced by most of these children increases the time homework takes, and to succeed in high school (and eventually at college), they need to develop the stamina to keep working. Consider it like training for a marathon—the marathon of life. NLD and Asperger's students carry a heavier academic burden than most people do, and they need to develop the strength to handle this burden.

3. **Find an appropriate place to study and make this the only place to study.** Keep in mind the guidelines described in chapter 7: no visual distractions or clutter, little traffic, and no noise. The space should be used *only* for studying, so, for example, it should not be in or on the child's bed. A note about studying in bed. Many NLD and Asperger's children experience sleep difficulties. Perhaps as a result of this, they are likely to want to study in bed. This should be discouraged: to make an area that is intended for sleeping available for studying can easily disrupt the development of good study habits.

4. **Set a stop time for homework sessions and stick to it.** This helps the child know that there *is* an end. For younger children, if the work is not done at the end of the study time, have a plan with the child to complete it later that day (if possible) or later that week. This is one reason why having the assignments for the week helps: you can plan ahead. If it happens often that the work cannot be completed within the week, speak to the teacher about the possibility of limiting the homework for a period of time to allow the child to catch up. In some classes this won't be possible, and as the work

piles up it creates anxiety for the child. At this point, you may need to discuss homework modification with the child's teacher. One way to modify homework is to have the child only do even numbered problems, or find some other way of reducing the work into less volume while keeping the same concepts. As these children mature and advance through the grades, this is less acceptable as a solution, as they miss material, find they will aren't progressing in their ability to tolerate increasing workloads, and feel inadequate in relation to their peers.

5. **Keep study segments the same on each study day.** For example, a fourth-grader has an hour and ten minutes set aside each day to adequately complete her homework. The first twenty minutes is devoted to math, then there is a break of five minutes for a drink and conversation with Mom, then twenty minutes for reading and vocabulary assignments, then a break, and the final twenty minutes for writing assignments. Each day, this routine is maintained, with the final twenty minutes being the segment that depends on the weekly assignments, which vary.

6. **Set a goal for each segment of study time.** Sometimes this goal will be to complete ten math problems, or to read to a certain page in a book, or it may be simply "studying."

7. **Take care of the logistics.** To do a homework assignment, the child needs to know what the assignment is before leaving school and be sure to have the materials. Use the support ideas mentioned earlier—a second set of books at home and a way to be sure assignments get home—to achieve this aspect of good study skills.

Staying on Task

It is important that adults supporting NLD and Asperger's students remember the issues specific to these disorders. These children's tendency to be distracted is real. Help them by using techniques such as providing a quiet place to study, or headphones to lessen auditory distractions. These students may not be attentive to detail—or may cling to the wrong detail; this is a serious problem. It means they will need to review their work with a parent, classmate, or mentor to be sure they have in fact done what was asked. Spell check and other technological aids can be useful and valuable to NLD and Asperger's students, although many ignore these aids.

Always remember that making mistakes is part of learning, not just part of these disorders.

By high school, the academic and social demands on these children will have increased to the degree that even students with high IQs are likely to experience difficulty. The trouble NLD and Asperger's students experience with multiple and complex directions can be lessened by requesting that instructions be simplified and assignments broken down into more manageable segments. Keeping a simple system of organization that allows the children to put papers and work in one place becomes even more important in the upper grades. Since staying on task during study time is also likely to be difficult, use multiple methods: a tape recorder, timers, pictures, or flashcards. Using self-quiz methods, asking others for help, and writing notes to themselves are all techniques that these students are likely to find most helpful in developing the study skills needed for upper level work. These techniques all make information retrieval less confusing. There are a number of excellent Web sites and books on developing study skills and more efficient time management tools. As the NLD or Asperger's student progresses to more complicated academic settings, incorporating such tools may be helpful.

Teaching Considerations

As we saw in chapter 6, nonverbal learning disability and Asperger's syndrome both involve failures in the executive function. The deficits that are most often seen are:

- Difficulty in planning

- Poor *self-monitoring* (keeping track of one's own actions and the effect they have)

- Expression of incorrect, impulsive responses

- Rigid behavior

- Failure to *complete an organized search* (that is, to solve a problem or search for an answer in a planned and organized manner)

- Poor *set maintenance* (knowing when ideas or concepts belong together—that math has different ideas and is different work from reading, though reading is often part of completing math homework)

With these deficits in mind, here is a brief list of points to remember when developing an academic program for the NLD or AS child. (An excellent source of further information for teachers is the book by Cumine, Leach, and Stevenson [1998] titled *Asperger Syndrome: A Practical Guide for Teachers*.) Although this list is hardly comprehensive, it will offer a good starting place for both teachers and parents.

- Always remember that AS and NLD are neurobiological disorders, and that dealing with the surface behavior will not necessarily correct the underlying deficits. These children will always have these disorders; what changes is the way they learn to handle them.

- In these children, *language level* does not represent *communication level*. Know the communication level of the child—that is, his or her ability to use language to interact.

- The academic program *must* include basic social skills. These skills include: listening, not interrupting, taking turns, sharing, waiting in proximity to others (i.e., in lines), and working with others. Learning these skills will take time.

- The AS or NLD child has to learn how to behave socially, and this learning is often stressful and time consuming. Academic learning may need to be seen as secondary for some children as they learn to function socially.

- A good teaching plan will include specific goals for developing skills in processing information. This plan will take into account the slow processing speed of these children and their need to be taught systems of organization.

- Be explicit and concrete in giving directions. Do not assume the NLD or AS child knows what you mean in a particular situation. For example, telling a child with AS to draw a card in a card game and "put that card in your hand" will not necessarily get that child to put the card with the other cards he or she is holding. Instead, the child is likely to simply put the card in his or her hand.

- AS and NLD children can easily become overstimulated and overwhelmed by auditory, tactile, or visual stimuli. This will impact what their classroom environment should be like, as well as the format and presentation of the lessons and worksheets presented to them.

- Check to ensure that the child is attending to the main topic, subject, or activity of the moment. Don't assume the child is focused on the correct topic just because he or she is on the correct page.

- Alert the child to his or her role in situations or tasks, making your description of that role concrete and explicit. This will be especially important in social situations where the child may tend to feel a victim, not seeing his or her own part in the interaction.

- Draw the child's attention to the use of gesture, facial expression, eye direction, and proximity in social situations. Develop "cues" to help the child notice the things he or she needs to notice to understand the meaning of an interaction. A *cue* is a prearranged gesture; for example, a gentle touch on the arm to remind the child to focus on the speaker's face.

- The concept of "pretending" is neither natural nor pleasurable for these children; keep this in mind when designing activities for them.

- Homework should be appropriate to the child's level and modified to increase the child's likelihood of success. A system of communication between home and school is essential, and the use of technology is highly recommended.

- The AS or NLD child often develops "expert status" on a topic of interest. Allow the child to utilize this competency with his or her peers and with you, but introduce ways to broaden the child's scope of focus. Keep in mind that over-focusing on a special topic may be comforting to the child.

Teachers should incorporate the following points into the curriculum for NLD and AS children, and they should be considered in all program development:

- Make the beginning and end points of tasks (assignments) explicit.

- Use checklists or a numbered series of prompt cards with pictures, diagrams, or scripts to help the child complete a task (including the task of getting through a school day).

- Provide a model of the final goal or end product. This can be a verbal description or (for the AS child) a picture example.

- Ask the child to repeat back to you what it is you want him or her to do, including the goal. Be sure the child understands what the goal is.

- Be clear, concrete, and explicit in directions and expectations.

- Design your program to explicitly teach ways for the child to connect knowledge from one area to another, providing opportunities for the child to generalize what he or she has learned.

- For the AS student, teach using sequences of visual cues; picture cards are one example.

- Focus directly on cause and effect, motives, and plot. These children are unlikely to see these connections without explicit teaching.

- When teaching social skills, offer the child explicit ideas on things he or she can do to navigate social situations. Help set up success situations for the child.

- Incorporating information from the field of *occupational therapy* can be very useful. These children's arousal states are usually poorly managed which interferes with their learning (more on arousal states in the next chapter). A team approach with an *occupational therapist*, a professional trained to work with sensory and motor skills, can be invaluable in this area.

9

Bodies in Motion: Addressing Deficits in Visual-Spatial Processing and Sensory-Motor Integration

In many cases—not all of course, but enough to pay attention to—the NLD or AS child was unique even as an infant and toddler. For parents, this child was the "good" baby—easy to entertain, not constantly "into" things, self-focused, self-comforting. There is another group of NLD and AS children who, as young infants, were inconsolable at times—seemingly overwhelmed by internal discomfort, and described as "colicky" by pediatricians and well-meaning grandmothers. Yet as a group these children tended to be content when read to or talked to, and as toddlers they often preferred quiet activities to wild and rambunctious games. Their reliance on using language to explore the world—asking "What's that?" instead of getting up and grabbing the object to feel and then perhaps eat—is possibly the first sign of their limited use of sensory-motor (physical) behaviors.

In normal development, children go through phases, often shifting focus among physical growth, language growth, and motor skill growth. Although there are no studies to date to support this idea, it seems logical that NLD and AS children find language and words much more comfortable than physical activities, and so their development in the area of language skills is self-reinforced—that is, language is more enjoyable and so it is returned to more often. It seems that the child comes wired, if you will, with a predisposition for difficulty with sensory information. The NLD or AS child is more likely to have problems with tactile sensitivity and auditory sensitivity and to have a highly sensitive and idiosyncratic sense of smell and taste.

Tactile Sensitivity

The feelings of the tag in back of a shirt or pants, the cloth of long-sleeved shirts, or of air on legs exposed through wearing shorts are annoying to the point of distraction for some of these children. Bathing in general and shampoo in particular—the "lightness" of the shampoo on the head—can be unpleasant for them. People standing close, perhaps in line at school or in the hallways, or the touch of a well-meaning teacher placing her hand on the child's shoulder: these are potentially unpleasant experiences for these children.

This acute *tactile sensitivity* can affect day-to-day functioning. For most of us, the relative roughness or smoothness of fabric or furniture, or the taste or feel of food, is noticeable, but it hardly interrupts our use of objects or our concentration on other things. But the way things feel, the sense that feeling creates for the NLD or AS child, is often enough to trigger a full-fledged meltdown. It is important to note that these meltdowns are not tantrums in the sense that a spoiled child has tantrums. They are more likely to indicate that a sensory overload has occurred and that the child's processing system is shutting down. The child has reached a point of being unable to handle the stimulation he or she is experiencing, whether it's the feel of the cloth, the feel of the shampoo, or the closeness of the other person. The explosion is the result of the overload.

Auditory Sensitivity

Auditory sensitivity is the child's heightened awareness of auditory stimuli. Sounds that are loud (or too loud for these children) or repetitive, such as the ticking of a clock or a classmate tapping a pencil or chewing gum, are grating and annoying to the point of being painful.

Jamie's Story

Jamie was eight years old when she began to notice that certain sounds in class were impossible to tune out. She had been schooled at home until now and had never really experienced a classroom of twenty-four students before. The ticking of the clock took her attention away from the teacher and the school announcement system came on in her class "way too loud" (in her opinion)—she had to cover her ears whenever the principal addressed the school. Classmates tapping pencils while they were working would annoy her so much that she had to ask the teacher to intervene. But all of these annoyances were nothing compared to the feeling inside her when people were chewing gum. The snap and chomp of the gum was like fingernails on a chalkboard to her. She could NOT stand it. The only time she received a suspension from school was the day she leapt from her seat and grabbed a classmate by the arm, yelling "Stop that. Stop that!" The classmate landed on the floor and Jamie was seen as the aggressor (which, technically, she was), all because this classmate was chewing gum in class. The teacher hadn't even noticed it and the student himself had not thought his gum chewing could possibly be such a problem. Jamie was not proud of her actions and the other students began to see her as a little "weird" after that, but, in her opinion, what else could she have done?

Sensitivity to Smell and Taste

Parents of an NLD or AS child will often report that their child has unusual food preferences long after the toddler years. Similarly, NLD and AS children will comment on how something smells— often when the rest of us can't tell anything special about the smell. It is interesting to note, though, that these same children will not notice when they themselves smell—which they often do because, as a group, they tend to resist bathing or changing clothes. Although these sensitivities have not been studied formally, such anecdotal reports are frequent and suggest that sensitivities for smell and taste may be as much a part of these disorders as those noted for the senses of hearing, touch, and sight (these children can also be over-whelmed by too much visual stimulus). The poor grooming that is so common in NLD and AS children may have as a source the fact that their sensory skills are askew, though it may also reflect their failure to notice that others notice them. (This second issue is one of social perspective, and will be discussed in a later chapter.)

Food Preferences

The food preferences of NLD and AS children are a well-known experience for parents of these children. Although these preferences are highly individual, anecdotal information suggests a general pref-erence for bland, pale, nontextured foods, especially "white foods": saltine crackers, bread, cream cheese, pasta, milk. Carbonated drinks seem to trigger mixed reactions with some children reporting that the bubbles are unpleasant and preferring juice or milk to sodas. This preference seems to be a part of the sensory wiring these children come with. In terms of intervention, it usually works best to offer the child more choices over the years, allowing the child's palate to mature. It is not useful to get into a battle over food. Provide several healthy choices, including some "white food" if that is the child's preference. Set a good example with the food the rest of the family eats and refrain from offering poor choices like fast food or sweets. These kids have enough going against them without adding poor nutrition.

Sensory Integration Techniques

The NLD or AS child's experiences of sensory sensitivity are real, and they affect the child's ability to attend, to concentrate, and to learn. The behaviors these sensitivities elicit affect the child's social relationships and sense of self-esteem. It is essential, then, that sensory integration training is part of any intervention these children are offered from an early age through high school.

Modulating Arousal States

The first intervention a child diagnosed with either NLD or AS needs is a complete assessment by a qualified occupational therapist. This is because no two children are exactly the same. This assessment will detail the work that most needs to be done with a child, and from the assessment a program can be developed that is tailored for the child. Certain programs, such as the ALERT program created by Mary Sue Williams and Sherry Shellenberger (1994), which most occupational therapists are trained in, have been very useful for NLD and AS children. These programs help the children learn to modulate their arousal states, allowing them to take in sensory information much more effectively. *Arousal state* means the level of attention and concentration we have at any time. Having low attention, or a low arousal state, is to be droopy and drowsy and easily distracted. Having high arousal is to be in an agitated, hyperalert state that makes us just as prone to distraction as low arousal. Without an ability to modulate his or her arousal states, the child swings from high to low and is likely to experience a meltdown. Using techniques to maintain attention and concentration without sensory overload, the child learns to avoid meltdowns and gradually develop ever greater coping skills.

Using Music

A music system with headphones (such as a portable stereo, computer, or disc player) has been a very successful intervention for many NLD and AS children. The music is predictable, and so the child's attention remains on the work in front of him or her. Clearly, this intervention is not appropriate for group activities or direct teaching time. When using this intervention, it is important that parents and teachers keep track of when the child is choosing to listen to music. There is a fine line between using music to maintain focus and screen out distractions and using it as a way to avoid social contact with others. The latter is not an option to be supported, and if it becomes a problem, intervention would have to be reevaluated.

"A Body in Motion"

There is a law in physics that says, in part, "A body in motion will stay in motion," unless that motion is interfered with. In the case of children with NLD and AS, not only does initiating movement not come easily, but keeping the body in motion does not seem to be the law that prevails. Instead, the NLD or AS child is likely to find himself or herself poorly suited for both large and small motor activities, especially activities that involve visual-spatial skills.

Teaching Fine Motor Skills

Tying a shoe is often difficult for the NLD or AS child. This task requires fine motor skills (fingers moving the shoelace) and visual-spatial understanding. In some ways it is like braiding: learning to braid (hair, yarn) is easy for some people, who just "get it," and close to impossible for others. As for shoe tying (or tying in general), do not start teaching this skill too early. Wait for the child's motor skills to mature, and use Velcro shoes until then. Just because your cousin Sally's daughter can tie her shoe at four years old does not mean your NLD or AS child needs to be able to do it at four.

When teaching shoe tying, or any motor activity, design a *script*—a set of verbal directions that help the child remember the pattern of the activity. Using language to support the motor skill will be more likely to help the child succeed. Also provide a *model* of what the finished product should look like: either a picture or an already tied shoe.

Teaching Balance

Bike, scooter, or other riding activities need balance and balance requires that multiple motor skills occur simultaneously. Such coordination is difficult for the NLD or AS child. Again, wait to teach this skill: you're not in a race to see which child learns the most activities first. Teaching balance first on a balance beam in occupational therapy or in an adaptive physical education class can add to the child's success. With patience and practice, the child can learn to ride a bike or other apparatus. Safety should be part of the teaching, and use of protective gear is a must.

Teaching Direction

As discussed, NLD and AS children actually tend to get lost more than other children do. This is a result of a couple of things: first their brains are not registering visual-spatial information the same way the rest of ours do; and second, as a group, these children tend to rush along, especially in situations that are unknown. When traveling along a path, most of us notice (to some degree) the way we came, and we are likely to be able to retrace that path. We use our memory of what we saw, heard, or smelled and our sense of the spatial relationships between things to help us remember how we got from one place to another. The NLD or AS child does not have this ability innately. He or she will need cues and verbal directions, and other specific help in remembering what to do.

At school, these children may need written directions or maps to help them learn the way from one place to another (from the classroom to the cafeteria or bathroom, for example). For some children, maps will be less useful, but counting the number of doors between the classroom and the bathroom will help. Landmarks should be pointed out: the big tree is in front of the office, the blue water fountain is next to the science room. In addition, the child should practice noticing the way and remembering the cues with a supportive person (only use a peer if that child is able to help the NLD/AS child with these cues). Cues might be landmarks (turn right at the water fountain) or small pieces of actual colored tape placed along the way to guide the child. Use the colored tape only for younger students, and train them to eventually use landmarks and verbal directions.

In public places that are novel, use of a walkie-talkie can help the child stay connected to an adult if the child wants to try and be more independent. This is a useful activity to help the child gain confidence in new settings, like the mall or public transportation. The parent or other adult trails at a distance and the child (with a peer, perhaps) practices getting himself or herself from one place to another. This activity increases the child's feelings of successes and reduces the sense of helplessness the child can feel in new settings.

Dysgraphia

Dysgraphia, or the inability to write, is a common disorder found in both NLD and AS children. Even the AS children who are good at drawing often suffer difficulty writing letters and words, or writing words on command. Writing is not the same activity as drawing, and just because a child can draw does not mean he or she can write well or fluently.

For some students, the writing itself—the formation of letters—is adequate, but it is slow and laborious. The effort required makes the act of writing unpleasant and the child learns over time to avoid writing. Many NLD and AS children will show significant discrepancies between their knowledge about a subject and their ability to write about the subject. Part of the problem is in the executive function deficits mentioned earlier, but part of the problem is in the mechanics of writing letters and words. Writing is a visual-spatial and fine motor task and because of that, it is very difficult for many students with NLD and AS.

Handwriting versus Keyboarding

As a rule of thumb, the early focus should be on mastering handwriting: printed and cursive writing should be undertaken, as with all students, beginning in kindergarten and progressing through the third grade. Cursive writing may be easier for these children as the spacing of letters is less of an issue, but the production of letters usually remains a problem. It is important that the teacher evaluate the particular problems the child is experiencing: desk height, the fit of the chair, and the posture of the student all contribute to success in learning in general and in writing in particular.

At a certain point, usually sometime during the third grade, the NLD or AS child becomes bogged down with the act of writing and his or her learning suffers. At this point it is a good idea to introduce the child to keyboarding, using either an AlphaSmart (which is like a small laptop but is only a word processor) or a laptop computer. Teaching younger students how to use a word processing program can alleviate the feeling of failure manual writing creates for them. Any classroom should be able to accommodate an AlphaSmart at the least. Students may eventually need to have their worksheets scanned into their laptops so they can work directly on the computer to complete assignments in math or other subjects. Software exists to facilitate this. What is also needed are faculty and administrators who have access to these products and are able and willing to use them. These simple accommodations can make a huge difference for the NLD or AS student, allowing him or her to keep up with the work in regular education classes.

Other Needed Interventions

Comfortable work positions and body posture are unique to each individual. In our cars we set the seat to suit us; in our homes we have a favorite chair or pillow. In classrooms across the country, desks are uniform and all students are expected to work in the same manner—sitting for long periods of time at these uniform desks. Most students comply with this requirement sitting and working as directed. But for the NLD or AS child, the desks and seats provided may actually hinder the ability to work and concentrate.

Help for Poor Posture

For reasons unknown at this point, many NLD and AS children have poor posture and poor muscle tone. Poor muscle tone requires specialized remediation, which will be discussed below. Poor posture clearly results from the child's poor muscle tone, but it also seems to result from the way the child uses (or fails to use) environmental supports.

A correct chair and a desk of the right height can make a huge difference. If there is a question, the child's occupational therapist can evaluate the furniture and make recommendations. In addition, NLD and AS children often work better if they are allowed to stand at their desk, to pace while reading, or even to lie on the floor or in a bean bag–type chair. These accommodations, along with rules for the child to follow, can be made in an elementary classroom without much disruption of the class. Use of special seating (T-stools for example, which are seats balanced on a single leg that the child must balance on) can be recommended by the occupational therapist, and can be a great help for the child in maintaining posture, attention, and work production.

NLD and AS children often have a unique and notable way of walking. There appears to be a great weight they carry around, causing them to hunch over, almost folding in on themselves. This posture conveys insecurity to less-than-well-meaning peers, and is often referred to as the "kick me" walk. Many of these children will either sit in a similar hunched over manner or lean back in their chairs, rocking the front feet of the chair off the ground and attempting to balance precariously on the rear legs. Their poor posture can eventually create real spinal development problems and should be corrected as soon as it is noticed.

Help for Poor Muscle Tone

Poor muscle tone describes the limp, noodlelike muscles these children seem to have. The problem seems to reinforce itself: the child begins with less muscle tone than normal, then finds sports harder or less pleasant than other solitary activities, and avoids them, so his or her muscles are not pushed. As time goes by, others the child's age become stronger and more accomplished at physical activities, and the NLD or AS child, feeling uncomfortable and unco-ordinated, falls further behind and is even less likely to want to try. These children's posture is affected, their stamina is affected, and their general physical health is affected. Establishing a program to develop these children's physical skills is as important as nurturing their mental skills, for without the posture, stamina, and muscle tone needed for learning, learning will be compromised.

The program should be developed by someone who is knowl-edgeable about proper form and the appropriateness of various activities for different age levels. For example, formal weight training needs to be taught by a trained professional and should not begin before the child is fourteen years old. Yet there are many weight-bearing activities that both build muscles and flexibility and can be taught at an early age. Carrying groceries in from the car, vac-uuming, and digging with a shovel all help build muscle control and flexibility and also include the child in activities that are part of daily life.

A physical training program for children should include:

- Warm-up activities

- Flexibility and stretching exercises

- Aerobic activities (plan for slow and steady increases in the amount of time the child can sustain an aerobic activity)

- Skill training for games and sports the child is likely to have to do (such as kickball, basketball, and softball)

Once the program is in place, a high school student or personal trainer might be found to serve as the child's coach.

A Final Word about These Interventions

Visual-spatial and sensory integration interventions are a necessary part of any program for NLD and AS children. Often, well-meaning professionals assume that these interventions are only valuable for young children, and so services or programs end when the child enters middle school. This is unfortunate, as the use of a trainer, of modified ALERT techniques, or of classroom accommodations for posture and dysgraphia are often needed throughout high school. Parents will need to advocate for their children and make services in this area as much a priority as academic services.

Social Competency: Issues of the Self, Others, and Self-Esteem

The Books

I read of fantasy
Of dragons and knights,
Goblins and ghosts.
I read of science
With ships in space and guns.
I read of mystery
Of murder and deceit,
Of trickery and lies.
I read of many things
Why can't I read your eyes?

—Lawrence Hsu, age fifteen
(*Sacred Grounds Anthology* 2001)

Throughout this book we have looked at NLD and Asperger's syndrome as disorders that have in common a deficit in the manner in which the individual takes in information and uses that information—an information processing deficit. It seems like a small thing, processing information. It is something we all do every minute of every day. But *because* we do it every minute of every day, it is hardly a small thing. The ability to successfully process information is central to an individual's ability to function in just about every aspect of life—learning, working, and having relationships of all kinds:

Information processing underlies

- The ability to learn

- The ability to function in the world

- The ability to be successful socially

In this chapter, we'll explore the effects of their information processing deficit on these children's social competency. Incorrectly judging the mood or emotion of someone else; not reading that your comments are boring or inappropriate; standing too close to others; avoiding responding to others because of sensory overload from information coming in: all these issues result from an information processing deficit and have negative effects on NLD and AS children's social success and, eventually, on their self-esteem.

Rachael's Story

Rachael is now sixteen years old. She is a slim brunette with NLD who has a loving nature and a naïve acceptance about her. She is often disheveled looking—although her mother takes great pains to buy her the latest "cool" clothes, Rachael never can remain looking put together. Rachael tells of her experiences in middle school and her first year of high school, where other children teased her for being messy and unkempt looking, for being weird and naïve, for being herself. She didn't shave her legs like most girls her age and the others called her "Monkey Girl." She came to view herself as "dumb" (especially in math) and "ugly" and would say these things about herself out loud to others. When asked why she did this, as it often resulted in more teasing or name-calling, she explained that it was what the other kids thought and she wanted them to know she thought so too. She wanted to be like them so that maybe they would be nicer to her. She had no friends and didn't expect to have any. She worried about her future. She began to sink into hopelessness and despair, becoming more and more depressed.

As Rachael's story illustrates, the effect of the information processing disability on these children's learning and social competency is notable, and not only in the obvious ways we have seen affecting functioning. It also has a significant effect on *self-esteem*, or the way in which the child views himself or herself. The inability to succeed socially and the frustration of experiencing social interaction as a foreign language eventually wear the child down. Over time, social failure translates into a loss of self-esteem that adds to the child's sense of confusion and isolation, and leads him or her to avoid social encounters. Eventually, if their social difficulties are left untreated many

NLD and AS individuals experience significant depression. Intervention in social competency is necessary before depression sets in.

What Makes It So Difficult to Connect Socially?

The NLD or AS child has real difficulty understanding the perspective of another person. Remember that these are children who have never really understood that others are thinking about what they think about and, more importantly, that others are thinking about them. This view of the world is, for lack of a better word, self-focused. That is not to imply that NLD and AS children have a callous disregard for the feelings of others or that their self-focus is self-centered and uncaring. On the contrary, they are very caring; they are just unaware that the views or needs of other people impact them. This awareness is not simple, and it does not seem to come easily for these children.

Looking in a Mirror, Looking out a Window

A self-focused perspective is similar to looking into a mirror and seeing only yourself. This worldview is quite different than looking out a window and seeing the world and the people in it. In some ways, it is as if NLD and AS children are caught looking into that mirror and our task is to get them to look out the window.

Addressing these children's issue of self-focus and their inability to take another person's perspective is a valuable goal, but in practice is difficult at best. If anything should be clear at this point, it is the idea that the three major areas of difficulties these children experience are all interconnected and affect each other. Given that the NLD or AS child is actually taking in information in a distorted way, it follows that any attempts to address their self-focus will be built on other interventions addressing their organizational deficits and visual-spatial deficits. Working on one area without addressing the other two is unlikely to be successful.

Noticing Other People

When the baby in his father's arms points to the moon and looks to his father, he is communicating with his father without language. The language of nonverbal communication—gestures, facial expressions, and body posture—is based, really, on a language of the eyes. Looking at the eyes of other people starts in infancy when we gaze into our mother's eyes. We begin using a kind of communication and interaction that transcends spoken language. It is interesting to note, as Simon Baron-Cohen does (1995), that even blind children will use language that denotes seeing, asking others to "look" at something— an act these children have never been able to do. The social meanings of looking and seeing are far-reaching, and the fact that NLD and AS children have a disruption in visual-spatial processing puts them at a significant disadvantage in interpreting the social communications that are based on seeing.

Learning to Notice

The first and most obvious aspect of social competency training for any child is practice in noticing things the child would not normally have attended to. For example, an NLD or AS child is more likely to hear a series of facts in a conversation with his or her mother than to notice that her hair is different, or her facial expression or even the tone of her voice. Further, given the limits of the child's information processing ability, a long monologue by mom is likely to be lost—jumbled and forgotten in the messy storage system of the child's brain. The fact that mom will repeat what she has said over and over to remind the child doesn't help matters (especially for mom, who becomes increasingly frustrated).

The child's inability to read the nuances of communication are very likely to lead to social rejection by peers and increasing isolation for the child. A look of sarcasm that is conveyed with the eyes, the knowledge that all the other kids have about how close to stand to someone, or the anger conveyed by the tone of the teacher's voice are all nuances of communication the NLD or AS child will miss. These nuances of communication will need to be taught. Again, it is important to remember that *language level* (how well a child can produce language) does not equal *communication level* (how well a child can communicate). We are interested here in helping NLD and AS children develop their communication level and, thus, their social competency. And the first thing the child will need to learn is to notice the important details in communication.

First Things First: Practice in Noticing

Practice in noticing should include both activities and direct instruction to explain the aspects of communication that are missed.

Parents and teachers should also create opportunities to help the child acquire the skills he or she needs to be successful.

Some aspects of noticing may seem obvious, some less so. To be successful socially, the child will need to learn to notice the many cues and messages that occur aside from the words people speak:

- Looking at other people's eyes. Ask the child questions about how other people use their eyes to convey information: Are they always the same? What does it mean when eyes are squinted, or wide open?

- Noticing where the person is looking. This is an aspect of shared attention, and noticing it assists the child in learning to read cues of meaning and to make assumptions.

- Noticing the expression on the other person's face. Ask the child to guess what it means: Is that an angry look? A worried one? A happy one?

- Looking at how someone is standing or sitting. Ask the child what he or she can guess about what the other person is thinking based on posture.

- Noticing how people walk—their speed and flow of movement. Ask the child what fast walking might mean, or slow, meandering walking?

Simple Social Skills: Not Easy, Just Less Complicated

Certain skills are central to social success, including noticing the behavior of others, discussed above. In addition to noticing, it is important that the child:

- Read the facial expressions and gestures of others

- Know their *own* facial expressions and what they are conveying *to* others

- Be able to have a sense of what is likely to happen in social situations—predicting outcomes lessens the novelty of interactions

- Keep in mind the presence of the other in conversation, and know that conversation is not a monologue

- Learn to give as well as learn to take. This is another aspect of taking the perspective of the other person. Giving and taking involve attention, compliments, and feedback.

For the child to regularly accomplish these tasks, he or she will need many years of organizational, sensory-integrative, and social skill training. A few ideas are listed in the box titled Practice Activities. But the best recommendation is to get involved with an experienced clinician—a psychologist, educational therapist, or behavioral pediatrician—who can manage the many aspects of this social skill training with the child. This person can be a valuable asset over the years to come.

Practice Activities

1. Videotape your child making a series of facial expressions: happy, sad, angry, worried, scared, bored, and so on, and have the child watch himself or herself. Do the same with other children and adults and have the child guess what the feeling is. This task can also be accomplished without a video camera: simply have the child make the face you request while looking into a handheld mirror. Polaroid photos can be very helpful; as the child practices and gets better at making the correct expressions, the photos provide a history of the child's progress. There are commercially made drawings of cartoon characters supposedly making facial expressions that match the word listed below the drawing. Although useful early in the development of social skills, the drawings are hardly accurate representations, and many children (and adults, too) would be hard pressed to guess what emotion some of those cartoons are supposed to be depicting.

2. Turn off the sound on the TV during a video or movie and work with the child to decipher what is happening. This will require that the child reads facial, posture, and gesture cues.

3. Read a story and ask "What do you think would happen next?" Discuss how important it is to have some theory of action—some way to predict what is likely to happen next. What cues give the child the idea of what will happen next. Learning to read these cues and predict action makes social situations so much less mysterious.

4. Create a book of situations, with different chapters for the different social demands the child will deal with that month, such as school, church, scouts, or a birthday party. Help the child predict what will happen and develop a plan for what they are likely to need to do in these situations. A formal program has been published that is

a more involved and well-developed variation on this idea: *Comic Strip Conversations* (1994) by Carol Gray. This is a very useful and well-thought-out program used to help children in just such a manner. It is especially useful for clinicians and school psychologists to use at a school site to help children deal with the social pressures they encounter.

5. Notice and work with animals. Working with animals is often less stressful and more fun for the child than practicing social situations with other people. What does that dog mean when he wags his tail? How about when he cowers down and puts his ears back? Contact with animals can be a wonderful way to work on empathy and reading social cues, as animals are predictable and engaging. Dogs in particular, as pack animals, have social behaviors that are easily described and learned. For the child, work with dogs can be highly positive, as most dogs (with a few notable exceptions) are forgiving of the mistakes a trainer makes and are happy to see the child.

At the Orion Academy, dog training is a required course for all students. This program teaches students to actually train dogs in good manners and obedience. The course spends a tremendous amount of time teaching the language of dogs—their development, their social hierarchy, and the meanings of their behaviors. The students use this knowledge to develop skills as trainers and handlers. The course is based on the idea that animals in general, and dogs in particular, have meaningful and complex social interactions and that they are actually easier to understand than people, so they offer a model for learning how to deal with people. To be successful as dog trainers, students must learn to keep track of the signals they, as handlers, are giving and at the same time read the signals the dog is giving. These are skills our NLD and AS students can use in day-to-day life.

Work with animals requires the guidance of a knowledgeable person, and dogs must be chosen for temperament and breeding. It is *not recommended* that an NLD or AS child be left alone *at any time* to deal with a family pet that is not screened or with an unknown dog. In addition to work with dogs, a number of programs for these children are including horsemanship. Horses, like dogs, are unlikely to be hurt by the child's mistakes, are smart, and generally enjoy being around people. Again, trained adults are necessary for these interventions to be successful, but access to this type of work should be available to more and more children.

Developing Skills in Social Competency

The process of developing skills in social competency usually develops over many years. As we have seen, beginning in infancy, skills of "mind reading" (Baron-Cohen 1995) and social connection are present. The first skills to be acquired are simple and straightforward. When someone says "hello," you are supposed to respond in a certain manner: for instance, look at the individual and say "hello" back. But soon even simple skills have more complex expectations associated with them. Greeting an adult requires a different set of expectations and a different set of knowledge about words, tone, and physical proximity than greeting an age-mate. The simple skills that the child starts with are added to over time, and more and more complex social interactions are expected by adulthood. For the NLD or AS child, movement from the simple skills he or she memorizes to the complex skills expected in adolescence and adulthood is a difficult task. Training and intervention in the language of social skills is a *primary* need for any program for these children.

For an excellent program in working with children in noticing and developing the social skills described here and in the next chapter, parents and professionals will find two books by Stephen Nowicki and Marshall Duke very helpful: *Helping the Child Who Doesn't Fit In* (1992) and *Teaching Your Child the Language of Social Success* (1996). These books offer ideas that parents can use and activities that can be incorporated into school programs and specialized activity groups.

There are many simple ways to develop opportunities for practice in social skills at both school and home, but a couple of general guidelines prevail. All children are more likely to work on and look at their own issues when working with someone other than a parent. No matter how close the relationship—and often because it is so close—children are reluctant to be totally open about their worries or their behavior with a parent. Social skill training is best undertaken and directed by a psychologist, whether at school or in a private practice. The parents should be involved in supporting the program through home practice. Speech and language therapists also make excellent partners for parents in working on pragmatic language development in individual and small group sessions. When parents take the time to develop a qualified team of professional and caring adults to help their child, the benefits are greater and the changes more significant.

The Concept of the Other

NLD and AS children need to develop an automatic response to check themselves—to notice what they are doing and the response they are getting. Becoming more aware of others reduces the tendency for these children to be seen as aloof and arrogant and helps them learn the language of communication that their peers take for granted. What they need to develop is primarily a sense of the other person in the interaction—an awareness of their audience. This brings us back again to noticing—specifically practice in noticing the following about *other people*:

- Their mood or feelings. For the NLD or AS child, the fact that others many notice that someone is sad without asking the person seems magic, like mind reading.

- Their expressions: does it fit the mood they are conveying through words and actions?

- Their posture: what is it conveying?

- Their spatial relationship to others. Is the other person close or far away? Does the other person seem comfortable with the proximity of the child?

- Tone of voice. Is the other person's voice varied or monotone, loud or soft? Ask the child to compare his or her own speech to the other person's. Does it have variations of pitch and volume in it?

- Speed of speech. What does it mean if another person's speech is fast or slow?

- Word choices. Is the speaker choosing words that are appropriate for peers when with peers and for other audiences (teachers, parents, work colleagues) when addressing them?

Developing Interventions for Simple Social Skills

For each skill or behavior to be taught, direct instruction will be needed, following the general guidelines (listed below). The model for teaching social skills follows these steps:

1. You explain verbally *exactly* what the child needs to do, developing a script, or set of verbal directions, if needed. For example, you'll use language to help the child understand what you mean when you say "facial expressions."

2. *Model the behavior*, or present an example of it using a picture, a video, or role play, so the child can see both how it should be done and how it should not be done.

3. Ask the child to explain to you what you just did. If you are using a script, ask the child to learn the script.

4. Ask the child to model, or demonstrate the behavior.

5. Develop a way to add the behavior to the child's memory. The type of information you're teaching will determine how best to help the child remember it. As an example, help the child remember that all behaviors for greeting and meeting people belong together by teaching them together, perhaps as a list or a rhyme the child can use as a mnemonic device, or by creating a book for the child. Social Stories *Comic Book Conversations* (Gray 1994) could be of help here as a way to create stories for the child's own situations.

6. The child must practice, practice, practice—with the adult, with peers, and in groups.

Building a Foundation of Social Skills

There are many social skills to learn and many aspects of any social encounter; that's why this process is so hard. But a few skills that are central to success can be identified. Recall the pragmatic language review form used at the Orion Academy that was presented in chapter 2. This form actually outlines many of the skills central to social success—skills most children master throughout their lives. In developing a program for the NLD or AS child, assessment of the child's social deficits and strengths should be first. Following that assessment, a coordinated and planned program of social training needs to be instituted. This program should take into account the developmental level of the child. The expectations for an eight-year-old in the lunchroom at school are very different from those of a seventeen-year-old in a similar situation. Keep in mind that skills need to build upon each other. You wouldn't ask someone who has never driven a car to drive to Los Angeles (even if you live there). You would teach the many parts of driving, then offer supervised practice, then, after success in less challenging and stressful situations, send the person to the freeways of Los Angeles.

So what are some of the simple skills ("simple" only in that they are foundation skills for more complex skills) that need to be mastered? An NLD or AS teen should have some understanding of all the skills listed here before he or she enters high school. For all of the skills listed here, make an effort to compliment the child when he or she does it correctly. Too often we are quick to point out when something is *wrong* and forget to point out when it is *correct*.

1. Looking into the eyes of another person when communicating. This conveys attention; it will also help ensure that the child is actually seeing the facial expression of the person who is speaking. Cueing the child to remember to do this will be necessary to help him or her remember, whether the child is practicing with a video or in a small group.

2. Using facial expressions that are appropriate to the content of the words spoken. Activities such as matching faces to statements on an audiotape and peer-to-peer practice are helpful in building this skill.

3. Noticing facial expressions, body posture, and physical proximity of the self and others. This training is best started in one-on-one practice sessions, moving gradually to work in small groups. Keeping track of all three areas (expressions, posture, and proximity) is much more difficult than any of the three alone, and increasing from one or two to more people in a group will increase the complexity.

4. Speaking clearly—not mumbling. For some children, mumbling is related to motor issues and needs to be dealt with in speech therapy; for others it is just a bad habit.

5. Using varied tone of voice and appropriate volume. The NLD or AS child frequently misjudges how loud he or she sounds and often forgets to make what he or she is saying interesting to the audience. Video- and audiotaping offer great feedback for the child.

6. Choosing topics for conversation that are appropriate to the setting (school, home, or other community settings) and appropriate to the audience (peers, adults, family, strangers). For many children, part of this training will involve developing separate lists of topics—one for school, one for swim practice or other social settings, one for home. These lists can become a safety net for the child in new or challenging situations. Practice with the child's speech therapist or psychologist in a small group setting to increase the child's feelings of mastery. This will help the child learn to call up the appropriate list on the spur of the moment.

7. Maintaining a topic in conversation. The child needs to learn to keep the flow on the topic and provide the necessary

information so others understand what he or she is talking about.

8. Flexibility in changing topics in a conversation. So often, the child will revert back to his or her preferred topic and need to be reminded of what others wish to talk about. This takes practice and feedback from adults.

9. Taking turns in a conversation—not monopolizing it.

10. Waiting to be acknowledged or called on before speaking in a group or in class.

11. Introducing oneself appropriately to others.

12. Using appropriate conversational pleasantries (such as, "It's nice to meet you," "How are you?", "Please," and "Thank you," etc.).

13. Asking for help when needed. It's hard to know when the chid needs help, as the child may not tell anyone, but providing the help needed and complimenting the child on asking for help are probably the best ways to increase this behavior.

All NLD and AS children need to have a program in place that addresses or will address, when age-appropriate, the skills on this list. Additionally, the complex social skills that we'll discuss in the following section should be part of that program. For most (if not all) of these children, a weekly social skills group will not be enough by itself. Their environment as a whole needs to support the development of these important skills. Often, it is helpful to arrange for a peer model for the child. In younger grades, the empathetic intervention of teachers who designate a buddy for the child can be very successful. This buddy presents a daily model (of sorts) for the child to emulate, while at the same time providing practice at social interaction. But by third grade, the buddy is often less interested in being responsible for the NLD or AS child—and frankly, it isn't the buddy's job to spend recess chaperoning this classmate. For children with greater needs in the social sphere—who also are prone to be "lost in space" and totally disorganized—assigning them an aide is often a necessary intervention. The use of an aide has its difficulties, as mentioned before, and aides should be used carefully within the context of a plan that will eventually eliminate their services. When any modification is developed for the child, the overall plan must include a transition away from that service or modification. If the child will need the service forever the plan should, consider how the modification will occur in adulthood.

Early involvement with peers and classroom education in tolerating diversity is extremely important for all children, not just the NLD or AS student. Yet this component education—an intervention at the level of the entire class or even the entire school—has limited usefulness if it's not followed up with direct teaching for the NLD or AS child. The responsibility for effecting change, the power to have control over his or her own happiness and success, needs to eventually rest with the child and not depend on the environment he or she is in. While this may seem like a minor statement regarding treatment approaches, this is actually an important concept. As mentioned before, the goal is not to create an individual who is dependent on the kindness of the environment for happiness and success, but to help the NLD or AS child mature into a self-sufficient and functioning adult who owns his or her own feelings and feels some level of competency in social relationships.

Complex Social Skills

Like mathematics, social skills build on each other. One skill, once learned, is added to making more and more complex social interactions possible. Most children handle complex interactions every day—holding a conversation, for instance. Conversations have purposes or goals, and the goal of one person may be different than the goal of the other. This means that getting needs met is one area of conversations that can be simple or complex. Asking mother for more potatoes at dinner might spark a dialogue—mother might ask if you "like" the potatoes. If you don't want to talk more you can convey this in tone, body posture, and facial expression as well as in words. This seems like a simple interaction, really. But the complexity comes in when you realize that mother worked hard on the potatoes. You want to compliment her, and you guess she is asking if you like the potatoes to check if you *will* compliment her. So you do. Now the interaction is more complex, and your goal has shifted from getting more potatoes to wanting to make sure mother feels complimented. Most of us never think about the layers of communication and meaning in conversations or interactions (sometimes no words are exchanged but a lot is communicated). Our NLD and AS children are at a great disadvantage here. If something as simple as wanting more potatoes at dinner can spin off so easily into other directions, just imagine what can happen with the many, many interactions we engage in daily. Talk about multitasking! We are constantly expected to organize multiple concepts and read different levels of communication at the same time.

Conversation skills and other, more complicated social skills develop over time, using the simple skills already described in combination and in sequence. Most NLD and AS children will need the same intensity of direct teaching for these skills as they need for simple social skills:

1. Being aware of the interest of the listener (not rambling on one topic). This is a complex skill as it incorporates many skills together—noticing verbal and nonverbal cues, organizing thoughts, modulating tone of voice, and flexibility in conversational topics, to name a few.

2. Introducing and discussing topics clearly, keeping the context and the connections between topics clear to the listener.

3. Expressing relevant information and expressing it concisely. Again, the child has to organize what he or she wants to say and to focus on that.

4. Attending to the comments the other person has made, responding to those comments, and allowing the flow of conversation to shift, if necessary. This last is a very important and often overlooked skill.

5. Understanding and using sarcasm correctly.

6. Understanding and using metaphor and analogy correctly.

7. Understanding and using teasing appropriately—responding in an age-appropriate manner to teasing. Not all teasing is bad, and learning how to tease friends is an art that can be acquired.

8. Letting go of an argument—allowing that the child may have to "agree to disagree" with the other person.

9. Learning to interrupt appropriately.

10. Learning to ask a speaker to clarify comments appropriately. There is a big difference between "Excuse me, could you explain what you mean by ..." and "That doesn't make any sense."

11. Being approachable for conversation—giving off the right cues.

12. Initiating original conversation; not talking about the same thing over and over.

Problems of Self-Focus

The idea of looking into a mirror rather than out a window is a way of understanding the problem of social interactions for NLD and AS children. It is not often discussed in the literature, but NLD and AS children and teens can appear to others as arrogant and self-focused. Their insistence on rigid rules and presentation of themselves as "experts" does little to increase their appeal in the eyes of their peers, and it can be annoying for family members. Well-meaning professionals and parents have often unwittingly supported these dysfunctional behaviors in an attempt to shore up the child's sagging self-esteem. While the need to support self esteem is real, allowing the child to present himself or herself to others as arrogant or self-important will neither shore up the child's self-esteem nor will it improve his or her social skills. All that happens is that another layer of problems is added to the child's already heavy burden of social deficits. It's a hard line for a parent to walk, helping the child feel good about his or her strengths in the face of difficulties while not feeding an apparent arrogance and sense of "specialness" that makes the child less likely to make friends.

Richard's Story

At fourteen, Richard considers himself an expert on all things related to his computer. He and his father spend many enjoyable hours fiddling with their home system and discussing the modifications they are making and plan to make. For Richard, these are pleasurable hours, and his father tells him over and over how smart and advanced in computer knowledge he is in comparison to his peers. Yet when Richard goes to school, his peers don't seem to notice how special he is. He acknowledges that many of the other eighth-graders in his class are better at sports, seem more organized, and have more friends, but he knows as much as they do about history and he is sure he knows more about computers. When he talks about his computer and the games he has downloaded, some students seem interested for a little while. But eventually they all seem to drift away, and Richard finds himself alone. He likes to give advice to the other kids to show them how much he knows, but there isn't a lot of opportunity and when there is, his advice is hardly welcomed. One morning, he came into his homeroom early to find his teacher, Mr. Smith, discussing his computer problems with another teacher. Richard intruded uninvited into the conversation and began to give Mr. Smith instructions on how to fix his problem. When Mr. Smith, who was annoyed by this behavior, replied "Thank you, Richard, but I have it under control," and turned back to the other teacher, Richard interrupted again to say "Well actually, Mr. Smith, I don't think you do." Needless to say, Mr. Smith was not inclined to find Richard's comment helpful or appropriate.

Being an "Expert"

Reliance on expert status is a common behavior for NLD and AS children and teens. They tend to have circumscribed areas of interest their entire lives, and they develop a certain expertise on the topics they have focused on for so long. It is important to note that although an NLD or AS child may have years of interest in insects, he or she may have a very narrow knowledge within that interest, perhaps having no knowledge beyond the special area of ants and beetles. Obvious problems occur when this expert status is pulled out and wielded like a weapon. This often happens when the child is feeling threatened or confused. Talking about his or her expertise has been pleasurable in the past and, like all of us, the child will seek to feel good whenever possible. Unfortunately, the child has little understanding of the effect this style has on the way other people see him or her. Sometimes, this syndrome has been made worse by well-meaning professionals or parents who have taken great pains to repeatedly tell the child how "smart" he or she is. Being as literal and concrete as most NLD and AS children are, the child interprets this literally, believing they that he or she is overall very smart and repeating this fact to others, whether it is appropriate or not.

Arrogance

Telling classmates he or she is smarter than they are or interrupting every conversation with "Well, actually," before launching into his or her ideas on the subject can make others view the NLD or AS child or teen as arrogant. In many ways, that view could be accurate, especially if the chid has never had help taking the perspective of other people, or has built up years of anger at the way peers have rejected him or her. The NLD or AS child is just as capable of being mean to another child as anyone is. Especially when these children are feeling confused or threatened, their limited social repertoire sets them up to use what they know—information. They have few weapons or defenses, and language is what they know best. This aspect of NLD or AS behavior is often ignored—the tendency to use an arrogant, better-than-you-are presentation to cover for feeling out of control and confused. The child feels a false sense of momentary control and has the sense of getting back at the kids who have been mean to him or her. This approach never pays off in the long run. The NLD or AS child really does not have control of the social situation and, worse, he or she tends to use this expert response even when not being threatened. This is a preemptive strike of sorts, as it has been explained by an NLD teen who assumes peers will reject him and starts out by presenting himself as above them to reject them before they reject him.

Unfortunately, many NLD and AS children and teens cannot tell when a peer is reaching out to them and often respond to gestures of friendship with this same arrogance. A potential friend must have a strong desire to be friends with some of these children to succeed. It is better that teachers, clinicians, and parents point out to the child when he or she is "doing the expert" and help the child change the way he or she interacts with others. The earlier this sort of intervention is begun, the better chance the child has of developing a range of relationship responses by adolescence. It will be to these children's advantage to be able to notice when someone wants to be their friend and to respond appropriately.

Fear of Letting Go

When it seems that other people have so much more information on so many day-to-day things, letting go of what expert status they have is a lot to ask of these children. It becomes the challenge for parents and professionals to strike a balance for the child, not taking away things the child needs without offering more appropriate replacements. In some ways, these children's need to cling to their areas of expert knowledge is not unlike the needs of a small child with a "blankie" he or she won't give up or a thumb he or she needs to suck. These ideas (or items) provide security, and it becomes very important for their healthy adult functioning that these children gradually learn to lessen their need for these things. It cannot be done quickly; just taking a computer away from a child who has relied on computers for years as an extension of himself will be devastating. His self-esteem is tied up in that machine, and moving him away from that position will take time. Conversely, it is not a good idea to allow these children limitless access to the material of their focused interests.

Broadening Interests

Try to help the child broaden the interest: a boy who compulsively readjusts the preferences on his computer could be urged (even required by his parents) to do more with computers that is outside himself. For example, he could set up a computer system for a neighbor or for a nursing home. He would not necessarily have to work with the people in these places, if that is too stressful, but he can spend time volunteering for someone else in the area of expertise where he is so comfortable. Help the child push his or her limits a little, and you might be pleasantly surprised. If you never expect the child to do things or take responsibility, he or she never will.

If attempts to help the child broaden his or her interests (for example, from an obsessive focus on steam trains to learning about the history of trains in the U.S. to eventually developing an interest in the history of the westward movement in general) do not seem to work, try to add interests. Expose the child to different activities and ideas, limiting the time spent on the obsessive activity. If computers are the obsession, limit the time on the computer each day. Insist that other things must be done to get time on the computer, and stick to that rule. For example, to earn an hour on the computer, the child would choose and do two of the following:

- Greeting mom and dad in an appropriate way in the morning and afternoon

- Bathing and grooming

- Brushing teeth after each meal

- Feeding and walking the dog

- Making pleasant dinner conversation

Parents can keep sheets of paper with these activities listed, and boxes beside the items to check them off. The child checks off each activity and presents the slip of paper, almost like a ticket, for computer time.

As the child matures, the checklist should contain activities that make more complex social demands on the child, such as participation in church, clubs, or after-school activities, or inviting a friendly peer over. It is very important to remember that although these children need some access to their security blanket (whatever that may be), if they are allowed to become immersed in their own world, it becomes harder and harder for them to participate in the world of other people.

Dashell's Story

Dashell loved history and would try to answer every question his fifth-grade teacher asked about American history. He would raise his hand and call out, "I know, I know," or sometimes just blurt out the answer before anyone else could. Other students were getting annoyed and would argue and become angry with him, seeing him as a conceited show-off. He had no idea he was seen this way, nor did his mom, until a parent told her how the other students disliked Dashell's style in class. His mother and the teacher talked to him openly about the problem, and he was surprised and worried—he was not trying to make the other kids dislike him. They devised a plan that was partly directed at Dashell and partly at the entire class. Dashell and any other student who wanted to could sign up as "contestants" in a twice-a-week classroom version of History Jeopardy (note this plan involves preplanning, which is important for NLD and AS children). The teacher specified the categories and the students played in teams, each getting the experience of being the expert. Dashell became a valuable and highly sought-after team member, and he learned to delay his need for attention and to listen to his classmates and value their responses. And he had fun!

Reliance on Rigidity

Left to their own devices, NLD and AS children will go through life like a train on a track: one way, straight ahead, never varying, avoiding the unexpected. Life doesn't allow any of us to live like this, so they need to learn to move off that track. Telling the child—and showing him or her through many experiences over many years—that *flexibility* is a good thing and not to be feared names the needed skill and helps the child learn it. Compliment the child when he or she is flexible, bending and changing and trying new things.

Avoidance of the New

The same technique helps these children stop avoiding novel experiences. It will take work on the part of parents to help these children develop skills at surviving in the world. Plan to take them places they might enjoy, such as restaurants, on public transportation, and to entertainment venues. The pressure to read so many pieces of sensory and social information at once is tiring and can be stressful, so don't do too many trips or arrange too many social encounters all at once. Increase the expectations as the child gets older. Like training muscles in the body, if you don't use social skills, you'll lose them, and the NLD or AS child needs to train for life.

Teasing and Being Teased

Perhaps the single most damaging effect of NLD and AS is the effect these deficits have on the child's social competency and on how others treat the child. Certainly, learning is impacted and without help the child's academic success can be compromised, but social rejection has devastating consequences. Teasing is part of life, right or wrong: there is hardly a person who has not been subjected to teasing at some point. "Friendly" teasing is often part of a rite of passage in some families—it shows you are an accepted member of the family when Uncle Joe teases you. It is also a common and accepted way of exchange between teenagers. The problem is that the NLD or AS child is so bad at it, that even when they try to tease, the experience is not usually positive. Eventually they just stop trying.

Playful teasing among peers is different from the painful and confusing encounters NLD and AS children experience on the playground or in social groups. From a very young age, they are often the subjects of comments and remarks from peers. This is partly because these children, as a group, call attention to themselves in less than admirable ways. Their gait, their odd manner of talking (the "little professor" speech), their poor motor skills—all mark them as different. In addition, the fact that many of these children are unaware of ordinary social expectations—much less the behavior that others see as "cool"—doesn't help. For example, for some reason that is difficult to explain, more than one NLD or AS child has had the annoying habit of nose picking in public. This behavior has a compulsive quality to it and the child will sit in class picking his or her nose, to the disgust of classmates. The teasing that predictably follows does not deter the child and he or she continues, losing social status and becoming the focus of ridicule.

Teaching Coping and Survival Skills

Not all NLD and AS children who are teased have a direct or observable behavior that can be addressed (like nose picking). Often the teasing stems from their misguided attempts to engage others, usually through their "expert" talking style, or just through not "getting" the flow of peer interactions. As mentioned earlier, it is important to provide as many healthy and supportive social situations as possible; it is also important to protect children from abuse or ridicule. Yet it will never be possible to control all the situations the child will encounter. It's better to equip the child with coping skills, which involve both strategies for looking at how the child interacts and good clear guidelines for reading a situation and judging if he or she needs to leave. Knowing how and when to leave a group is just as difficult as knowing how to enter one. Unfortunately, many NLD and AS children wait too long before leaving a social encounter gone bad. They have poor judgment and limited ability to read social cues, and can easily get themselves into hurtful or even dangerous situations. Social skill training should include teaching ways to get out of a situation that is making the child uncomfortable.

Knowing how to *avoid* situations that are likely to be problems is another valuable skill. For example, if the bathroom in C wing of the local high school is the hangout for the "tough" group of girls at lunch, teachers and parents need to explicitly tell the NLD or AS teen that she should not go into that bathroom. The social skills needed to handle the potential problems there are more than this girl has at her disposal. Teaching survival skills involves teaching children that everyone is not necessarily going to be their friend. This teaching requires that NLD and AS children are not so protected that they never learn how to survive. The more they get out and learn scripts for handling life, the better able they will be to live it.

A word of caution is in order here. As easy as it may be to say that you must teach survival skills, there is a very fine line to walk here. The challenge for parents and professionals is to strike a very important balance, providing a safe and supportive environment for these children without overprotecting them from life. A safe and appropriate educational environment is a must; this is not a need that can be ignored. And the child will need to be allowed to try things, to succeed and to fail socially, with the knowledge that his or her family is there as support, always.

Putting It All Together

For the NLD or AS child, just like for any child, success finally boils down to the child's ability to put it all together: all the assessments, the focus on developing social and organizational skills, the experiences and arranged practice. Putting together what we've learned allows us to function independently in the world. It involves defining what makes us happy and setting out to achieve that happiness. Who could ask for more, really? Even for children with no disability, finding happiness is not necessarily an easy thing. This book attempts to show how complex are the interactions most people take for granted, and how they require a complexity of social and organizational skills. Understanding nonverbal as well as verbal communication is essential for this functioning. According to Duke, Nowicki, and Martin (1996), "Only 7 percent of emotional meaning is actually expressed with words" (7). That means that 93 percent of the emotional meaning in the way people communicate is expressed in ways other than spoken language. To miss 93 percent of the meaning in an interaction is a serious deficit. With this in mind, it should be clear just what level of hard work NLD and AS children and their families must go through to develop skills others take for granted.

Learning how to use words to their advantage is a goal most NLD and AS children can eventually reach. Learning how to connect the nonverbal parts of communication with the verbal is also something that eventually can be accomplished. This work is necessary and central to healthy development, just as central as academic learning. Being accepted by peers and adults in your community goes a long way toward fostering healthy self-esteem. Instead of a false sense of self-worth, created artificially by the adults in the child's life, developing real competency in social situations is a valuable and reasonable goal. To develop this competency, the lessons of the past chapters are important. In addition, these children need to develop a total package of skills that defines who they are and reflects the view of themselves they want others to have. This view involves as a direct result of the work in taking another person's perspective. It is a natural extension of the sense of self, and NLD and AS children need help making this extension.

Who are they and how do they want others to think of them? This is a hard question for most NLD and AS children—and most teens, regardless of disability—unless they have been working directly on this idea. To answer the question, they first have to think about themselves as they relate to others; they have to think about "others" as they relate to themselves. Most children never think about this idea as consciously as every NLD and AS teen will need to at some point in their lives. Answering those questions is important and complicated, and the ability to do so develops out of the hard work described in this book.

Being "Cool"

Ask any child what "cool" is and he or she will be hard pressed to define it in words. More likely, the child will give examples of what *is* and *is not* cool. In essence, "cool" is knowing and using the correct connections of word choice, tone, flow, and rhythm. It is being aware of and in tune with the situation and interacting appropriately with those around you. In clinical terms this awareness is often referred to as *synchronicity*. Developing a synchronicity with those around you suggests you know how to use nonverbal communication, that you can read much of that 93 percent of the communication that is not spoken. Developing synchronicity makes you cool.

Grooming

Another level of communication, described by some as *objectives* (Duke, Nowicki, and Martin 1996), is conveyed through things like posture, tone of voice, rate of speech, and general body language. Part of that body language that appears to be a particular problem for NLD and AS children and teens is grooming. As mentioned earlier, poor hygiene appears partly to be a result of the sensory integration difficulties these children experience. The feel of water, shampoo, or a toothbrush is so disturbing to them that they learn to avoid the experience. The fact that they cannot smell themselves or notice that their clothes are stained and rumpled from days of wear complicates matters. So parents, professionals, and other caretakers need to begin early teaching the child that the social conventions of our culture require a certain level of grooming with which they must comply.

Be creative: pants or skirts with elastic waist for young children can usually be found to accommodate any situation. Set a schedule for bathing and hair washing and stick to it; this will develop into a routine and become easier. Keep in mind that if you wash it often (say, every two days), the child's hair will require quicker washes, which will in turn increase the likelihood of the child's accommodating to the feel. Experiment with different shampoos and soaps, and add fun to bathing whenever possible. As for older children and teens, you can't wash them, so you are left with the old standby: washing earns them privileges and rewards they desire. It is necessary to teach this life lesson—that stinky people are not easily accepted by peers.

Here's an example of how this lesson can be reinforced.

A parent refused to drive her son to school in the morning because he had slept in his clothes for three days in a row and had not bathed. When he got up in the same messy, rumpled outfit for the third day, she told him to shower and change, and only then would she take him to school. He refused, stating he would just stay home then. The mother, no dummy she, called the school, got his teacher on the phone, and explained the situation. The teacher told him that she understood the problem and what his choice was, but that he would be counted as "cutting" for the day and she hoped to see him tomorrow. His mother told him to go back to his room after he had eaten and that he would have no TV or computer privileges because he cut school. Later in the day, his mother reminded him of the need to shower and be dressed in clean clothes in the morning, and said she would not get into a debate with him about it. This was the rule and she intended to stick to it. The next morning, he was showered and dressed in clean clothes.

This is not to imply all such encounters will go so well, and some children may need more than one experience to get the message. But this type of situation has been played out many times and a few points seem to increase success:

- Be clear and concise in your expectations. Don't say one thing on one day and another thing a different day. In the example just given, the mother sent a clear message: you need to shower every two days and wear clean clothes to school. *Clean* clothes were defined as having been worn no more than two days and not slept in.

- Stick to your guns in a calm and businesslike manner. There is no reason to scream and yell. Remember that the child is responding to his or her internal states and the learning he or she has already taken in. In most cases that learning has been that the parent will give in. But if the child stinks, he or she needs to bathe or he or she cannot continue to enjoy privileges. It is a logical consequence: the smell or inappropriate clothing disrupts others, and for these children, learning the effect they have on others is very important. Remembering the importance of this leaning may help you stand firm.

- In the example given above, the parent solicited support from an important person in the child's world—his teacher. This was a valuable intervention, as the teacher presented a logical consequence the child understood—he was cutting school. The teacher was not angry nor was she pleading or cajoling—like the mother, she was clear and businesslike, explaining what the consequence was.

- Remind, but don't nag. Offer ideas of how the child can do what he or she needs. Offer options for shampoo, soap, or bathing methods.

Compromise and negotiation may also be needed in the matter of clothing. Most NLD and AS children have a defined style they prefer. This style may be compulsive, like a jacket that *never* comes off, even in hot weather. There is room for personal style, unless the child attends a school with a uniform, and then he or she must comply as required. If there's no such restriction, having five different pairs of sweatpants for school may be boring, but it will be clean and neat, and it can allow the child to dress in a manner that is a compromise between his or her sensory needs and society's demands.

Issues of Adolescence

For older children and teens, the issues of coolness and grooming are a bit more complicated. Given that most NLD and AS teens are developmentally behind their peers, they often don't even notice what is "cool" in clothing. For some parents, especially if the NLD or AS child is their first child, the temptation is to keep dressing the child "younger" than is appropriate for his or her age or grade. This may be due to the child's not requesting a change of clothes, or the parent's just not thinking about it, but a fourteen-year-old in Gymboree shirts (even if she can fit into them) is not a good idea. As a rule of thumb, middle of the road dress makes the most sense for these children. That is, it would not be a good idea to dress the NLD or AS preteen or teen in eye-catching or seductive clothing, including expensive footwear for boys, even if all the child's peers are wearing it. The attention those clothes may draw may be more than the child can handle. Think simple, comfortable, and easy to wash.

Just because a child has NLD or Asperger's syndrome does not mean he or she will skip being a teenager. No, the child is just as likely to go through the normal variations of mood and personality as any teen: he or she just gets to go through adolescence with more baggage. The good news is that, developmentally, most of these teens are slower to become aware of adolescent issues of sexuality, drugs, or rebellion, but these issues will come up. The NLD or AS teen's logical mind can be a help here. The peer culture we want these children to become a part of is difficult at best, and many of our NLD and AS teens are not prepared to deal with the pressures of sex or drugs. The best approach is to arm the child with information and a plan beforehand and, most importantly, to teach the child to talk to an adult if he or she has any questions or confusing encounters. There is no way parents or professionals can prepare the teen for every possible scenario that will come up. Instead, the child needs to know that the best course is to get away from confusing situations and talk to adults he or she trusts. Drugs and sex need to be introduced into these children's school curriculum just as for any teen. They need the same tools and information, but these tools may need to be introduced one-on-one or in smaller group settings with ample opportunity for questions that their peers might find weird or unusual.

The typical adolescent rebellion, or the *separation-individuation phase* of adolescence as it is known clinically, is alive and well for

NLD and AS teens. The phase usually happens later (at age seventeen or eighteen, instead of fifteen or sixteen) and it may look different, as the NLD or AS teen is genuinely frightened about what the world has to offer. The idea of leaving home may be overwhelming to these teen, yet their developmental need to achieve some separation from their parents is real. This confusion can be the source of depression and hopelessness in later adolescence and may need to be addressed professionally.

Closing Comments on Self-Esteem

What is self-esteem but the development of a healthy sense of who we are? No one is perfect, and knowing our limitations along with our strengths helps us accept what is real about who we are. Developing a false sense of ourselves is unhealthy and dangerous. This is just as true if that falseness defines us as worthless or as extraordinary. For NLD and AS children, growing up is a difficult and confusing journey. They begin the journey knowing only part of the language and having only part of the map and part of their luggage. Self-esteem comes with the knowledge that they can succeed, even if that success relies on the help of others. There is no question about the many deficits these children struggle with, yet the strengths they come with are also valuable and worthwhile to them and to those who know them. During the trip they will need help and support to find the missing pieces, but it is ultimately their journey.

11

What Does the Future Hold?

As this book draws to a close, some issues remain untouched and some ideas unfinished. Recall that nonverbal learning disability is a relatively new diagnosis and because of that it has been underdiagnosed, misdiagnosed, and just plain misunderstood. Exactly what NLD is has yet to be defined in any consistent manner, and as discussed previously, the name itself doesn't do justice to the real issues confronting the individual. In this book, Asperger's syndrome has been considered in conjunction with NLD. Although it is a recognized DSM-IV diagnosis that is accepted in both the education and mental health fields, AS is also frequently misdiagnosed, creating confusion and difficulty in research and in program placement.

This book presents one view about NLD and AS; there are others. The conclusion presented here is that although they are separate disorders, NLD and AS should be considered *related* disorders. Both have in common the problems of information processing that affects organization skills, executive function, sensory integration, and social competency. As related disorders, they appear to respond to similar interventions and educational programs. The exact nature of the relationship between the two diagnostic categories is unclear, yet it is possible that they belong together on a continuum and that that continuum is separate from the autism spectrum disorders. This idea remains to be proven and for now, most people still consider AS an autism spectrum disorder and often refer to AS children as autistic. This book takes issue with that notion, but only future research will provide the knowledge to develop a consistent understanding across different fields of study.

A Better Than "Just Getting By" Approach

To date, professionals trying to work with NLD and AS children have relied on a limited body of information, some of which has been primarily anecdotal. There is a slowly growing body of empirical information to back up the commonsense ideas and observations much of the past work has been based on. Up to this point, parents have been left with interventions that feel like a "hit or miss" approach to addressing their child's needs. Most parents are actively seeking knowledgeable professionals, who can help their NLD or AS child to reach his or her highest potential and have the greatest opportunities for the future. According to a study originally published in 1993 and reported in an article titled "The Epidemiology of Asperger Syndrome: A Total Population Study" by Ehlers and Gillberg (www.asperg.org 2001), it is estimated that the prevalence of AS is 2.6 per 1,000 individuals. With the population of the U.S. currently estimated at 275 million (July 2000), this would mean an estimated 715,000 people are affected by Asperger's syndrome in the U.S. alone. The estimates for NLD reported by Rourke (1995) are 1 out every 10 learning disabled individuals (or 1 percent of the general population), or an estimated 2.7 million people affected by NLD in the U.S. alone. This means that approximately 3.4 million people in the U.S. are affected by these neurobehavioral disorders. Diagnosis and treatment should be a high priority for mental health and education professionals.

A recent article by Philip Hilts in the *New York Times* (2001) cited a report by the National Academy of Sciences suggesting that school systems should try to diagnosis autism as early as age two. With earlier diagnosis, the number of children identified with autism and related disorders and needing services at schools will increase, as will the pressure to find effective treatment programs. It is likely that many of the children diagnosed with autism and related disorders are in fact AS or NLD children who will need services specific to their disorders. An increase in knowledge regarding both AS and NLD will allow for greater accuracy in diagnosis and, eventually, more appropriate program placement.

Effective Program Development

Program placement and related services for NLD and AS children have been inconsistent at best and ineffective at worst. It is essential that an intervention program be effective—it really is just common sense. If something isn't working, it is hardly worth continuing. The same is true for all aspects of education and any type of treatment. The failure in treatment effectiveness for NLD and AS children can be traced to the following basic problems:

1. Poor diagnosis of the disorders. The child is often not even receiving the necessary treatments: educational, speech and language therapy, occupational therapy services, or appropriate medication.

2. Use of adjunct services in lieu of an overall program approach. A program approach means that the educational curriculum is based on an understanding of the specific needs of children with information processing deficits and that the classroom incorporates the interventions into the total program. Interventions for information processing deficits need to address three major areas:

   • Organizational skills and executive function

   • Sensory integration

   • Social competency

   To provide services once a week or as add-ons, afterthoughts to the main program, is to provide services that are unlikely to create any substantial change.

3. Failure to develop and use modifications that change over time, allowing the child to grow toward independence and self-sufficiency. A child with NLD or AS should have different modifications in fifth grade than in eighth grade, and by high school should be progressing toward fewer modifications or toward using technology that the child can reasonably take into the adult world. Technology can be a great asset for these children, and informed use of new and innovative technology should be a priority in programs designed for them.

Program development should include the points addressed in chapter 8 and in appendix C, the Classroom Wish List. Any program for NLD and AS children must include organizational skills training and training in the use of technology as parts of the program, not as add-ons. Recall the use of the whiteboard technology that allows direct transfer of information from the board to the student's laptop. This classroom modification reduces the multitasking requirement present in more advanced subjects, allowing for greater comprehension and more involvement in the material and the classroom discussion.

An appropriate program must take into account in a real way the sensory integration and visual-spatial needs of these children, from classroom design and the availability of different sensory integration tools in the class to development of appropriate educational materials. Teachers and administrators need to be aware of the sensory integration needs of these students and make available appropriate desks, chairs, headphones, or other items the students can use to maintain appropriate arousal states.

The curriculum and social climate of the program must include training in social skills. A central focus of any intervention program for these students must be teaching pragmatic language, self-observation, and the ability to adopt another person's perspective. Traditionally, NLD and Asperger's children have participated in pragmatic language training programs, usually in small groups run by a certified speech therapist. These groups are similar to social skill groups run by licensed psychologists, and they focus on developing the child's ability to use language appropriately and develop behaviors that are socially acceptable. These children's success while in the group is usually high, and the experience is a valuable one. Yet, as mentioned earlier, most professionals find that the skills developed in the group do not generalize easily outside the group. It is a problem worth further study.

As discussed in chapter 10, some success has been found in dealing with social issues using animals—specifically dog training—as a means to develop skills in reading cues and responding with self-awareness. The purpose of a dog training program is to teach the students to "read" the dogs, learning how to respond and give appropriate praise and corrections to the animal in their charge. More research on successful intervention in social competency is needed, as this area of work is difficult and often frustrating for the student and the teacher or therapist.

The Swing of the Pendulum

Attitudes about education in general and special education specifically seem to follow a cycle that's like the swing of a pendulum. Not only do diagnoses seem to come into and go out of fashion, but certain concepts in education seem to go in and out of vogue as well. For the past fifteen years, the pendulum has swung away from specialized education and into the popular idea of "mainstreaming." *Mainstreaming* is the concept that special-needs children should be taught in the mainstream of education—in regular classes or in regular education settings—as much as possible. It sounds good, and it has had some benefit for the group of children who were being isolated and not offered an adequate education in special education. But for a large number of children, the effect of mainstreaming has been a loss of the specialized classrooms and teachers trained to provide the program (not just the tutoring) they needed. Districts experienced a financial gain by limiting special education services. For NLD and AS children, mainstreaming is hardly enough, and real program changes are needed. They need specific types of materials, access to computers, and direct specialized teaching for executive function and organization, pragmatic language and social skills. Their needs require a shift in thinking from a regular education classroom.

A lack of appropriate services and of general knowledge about NLD and AS has started the pendulum swinging back. Within the last few years, parents seeking services for their children have fueled the growth of information about and interest in NLD and AS. At times, the services provided have not been in the child's best interest—for example, the use of an aide throughout a child's academic career is hardly preparing the child for increased independence and academic success. The plan for that child needs to include program changes as the child matures and direct teaching and technology geared toward helping the child become a teen who is more self-sufficient. It is time to reach a balance between extremes: providing specialized services that are academically challenging and not limiting to the student socially or academically. It is time for professionals to get interested and develop programs that specifically address these children's issues. Research on and funding for these programs is badly needed.

Effect on Families

One of the hardest things this book is asking families of NLD and AS children to do is to allow them to fail. The swing of the pendulum that fuels increased services can also protect these children from normal development—from the frustrations and pain of everyday growing up. Clearly, for a parent this is the hardest line to walk: allowing some failure to support development of inner strength, but protecting the vulnerable NLD or AS child from becoming overwhelmed by life's trials. Families have the extra burden of finding that line on a daily basis and trying to walk it as best they can. There is no doubt that these children need protection, that they cannot be set out to walk in the wilds alone without training, practice, and preparation. It is that training for life and practice in surviving that is essential, and is often overlooked. To assume that the NLD or AS child will never be able to go on a bus alone or complete a job interview or deal with the DMV is to assume less of them than they are capable of.

Family members will provide a backup system for the NLD and AS individual for that person's entire life. Part of the training that is needed is to teach these children who will be adults someday when to ask for help and when to let others know they can do it themselves. Specifically, NLD and AS children need to be educated in their disability and become involved in their own treatment. Developing good working relationships with their psychologist, psychiatrist, and/or their medical practioner will provide much needed support over time. These relationships can continue throughout the lives of NLD and AS individuals and can provide an alternative to parental advice that can be especially valuable as they move into young adulthood.

Qualification for Special Education Services

The school system is an essential partner in the success of any child, and that is no different with NLD and AS children. Most NLD children who qualify for special services will do so under categories related to their disability but not specific to NLD.

Every school district in the country is required to provide special education services and meet the guidelines of PL-94142, the federal special education law that went into effect in 1976. But each school district has the ability to interpret the law, and many states have included additional requirements for special education services. As mentioned earlier in this book, parents must take the time to find the laws in their state and the guidelines for their district. Yet a parent can request that his or her child be evaluated for special education at any time, and that evaluation must occur in a timely manner. If the district concludes that the child does not qualify for special education, the parent may disagree, and has recourse through mediation and a fair hearing process. Keep in mind that this can be a long process; many families find the stress difficult to deal with alone and seek the services of an educational attorney or advocate.

NLD is not a recognized diagnostic category, and a diagnosis of NLD will not automatically get a child special education services. Yet many NLD children are in serious need of specialized service and program modifications. In some states, services that are not part of an IEP are still available. In California, for example, many NLD children qualify easily for a *504 plan*. This is a state-mandated program that provides services for students who need modifications to their educational plan but do not qualify for an individual education plan (IEP). The IEP is a legal document that defines the educational program for any child who qualifies for special education services. The 504 plan is implemented at the discretion of the school district and monitored at the school site. Because it is not an IEP, a 504 has limited accountability, and frankly, services provided are at the convenience of the individual school. Most 504 services are ones that do not cost the district any additional funds—for example, preferential seating in the front of the room, but not purchase of a special desk for the child.

Depending on the state and the district, qualification for special education often requires focusing on specific deficits or specific learning disabilities—written language, mathematics, or pragmatic language development—or on the discrepancy between potential skills (as measured by testing) and actual performance. Many parents of NLD students have required the services of an educational attorney to get their child the accommodations and program the child needs. But there are success stories, and plenty of district staff who are interested in providing quality programs.

Assessment

The first step in designing a program for a child with NLD or AS is to get a good assessment. From the assessment, teachers and case managers will develop the modifications that are needed, the specific training and teaching tools to be employed, and the additional services to be provide (such as speech therapy, a social skills group, or occupational therapy). Throughout this book, ideas and suggestions for just what that program should look like have been presented, but no two children are alike and each program will need to take into account the individual needs of the child and the family.

Transition into Adulthood

NLD and AS individuals' transition into adulthood is probably the least understood part of their lives. Programs have just begun to catch up on services for children and teens; there are as yet almost no services for young adults. The junior college system can offer continued special education services until age twenty-two, and is a potential avenue for help. Yet, little is specifically available. Web resources like NLDline.com and NLDontheWEB.org offer bulletin boards, chat, and links for NLD individuals to make connections and suggest things that have worked for them; OASIS.com does the same for AS children. Common sense and experience with NLD and AS teens suggests that continued support will be needed for many years and that helping these teens prepare for the demands of adulthood will be very necessary.

Future Research

NLD and AS are disabilities that affect many families every day. Research on both is underway and needs to continue if we are to develop effective programs and better assessment practices. Professionals who are struggling to define these disorders need to communicate their ideas and experiences, sharing what they know or think they know. For now, we are left with many ideas, many possibilities, and many opinions. At the beginning of this book, I noted that it is possible that in the years to come the ideas presented here could prove to be useful or not: for now, they are a place to start. Future research will offer us all information to help define the disorders, refine our work, and enhance our success with our NLD and AS children.

12

Resources and Program Planning

NLD and AS children are a treasure and an asset to their families and to our society. Their potential is unknown, and often untapped in traditional educational settings. As we have seen throughout this book, special programming is needed to allow these children to overcome the limitations their particular disabilities present. NLD and AS children will need intervention in their day-to-day lives, beginning with early diagnosis and program planning. The planning must include a long-range vision of how to move the child toward greater effectiveness and away from helplessness and a self-definition as a weak, incompetent person or an invalid.

Knowledge Is the First Step

Knowledge empowers people, and gaining knowledge about NLD and AS is the needed first step for families, the professionals who work with the child, and the child himself or herself. Families in particular need all the information they can get. Professionals need to receive training in handling and providing services for these children. The children need to understand their disorder—to know it is not a mystery and they are not so weird. There are many children like them who struggle with the same issues. The Harry Potter books, by J. K. Rowling, are particularly popular with NLD and AS children (and other children too, of course). One of the reasons NLD and AS children love these books is their presentation of a boy who is born different and who doesn't fit in, but who learns about himself and discovers the magic within him. For NLD and AS children, this discovery process is essential, and it must be guided by knowledgeable adults.

Assessment and Evaluation

As noted throughout this book and outlined in appendix A, a competent and complete assessment is essential for appropriate and accurate program planning. The program that results is likely to include:

- Educational modifications

- Occupational therapy

- Pragmatic language training

- Social skills training

Many NLD and AS children will also need medication and ongoing work with a psychiatrist and psychologist.

The Educational Program

Given that school-age children spend more of their waking time in school than at home with parents, the program at school is very important. Children diagnosed by a medical doctor or psychologist with AS frequently qualify for special education services early and have an individual education plan (IEP) in place early in their academic careers. This is not necessarily true for children with NLD. The U.S. Department of Education's Office of Special Education and Rehabilitative Services lists twelve categories of special education, including specific learning disabilities, speech and language impairment, other health impairments, and autism. Each school district is responsible for implementing special education programs and is also responsible for providing the services and meet the goals defined in a student's IEP. Development of the goals for the student and the decisions about appropriate program placement are decided at an IEP meeting, which is attended by parents, school district personnel, and anyone invited by the parents. The IEP is drafted at this meeting. The usefulness of IEP is determined by who contributes to it, and because of this it is important that the parents include knowledgeable professionals on their team. Parents have a right to have anyone they wish on the IEP team, and they can present the IEP goals they want to be included. A good assessment comes in handy in helping them determine these goals. Attorneys or other trained advocates for parents are often necessary to set up a working document that is appropriate for NLD and AS children. Many school districts and private schools know little about NLD and AS and will need information provided to develop appropriate programs. If the district is unable to provide the educational environment the child needs to benefit from his or her education, the parent has every reason to seek private services for the child and engage the district in a discussion about how they will provide those services.

Internet Sites

The following Internet sites have information and resources that can be extremely useful to parents and professionals interested in NLD and AS.

For nonverbal learning disability, the following two sites are excellent. The Nonverbal Learning Disability Association (NLDA) is a national organization that offers information and support for individual and families with NLD and can be contacted through the NLDline.

- www.NLDline.com

- www.NLDontheWEB.org

For Asperger's syndrome and related topics, these sites are great places to start. They offer comprehensive information and links to other sources of information.

- Online Asperger Syndrome Information and Support (O.A.S.I.S.): www.udel.edu/bkirby/asperger

- Yale Child Study Team: www.info.med.yale.edu/chldstdy/autism/index.html

- Asperger Syndrome Educational Network (ASPEN): www.aspennj.org

- Asperger Syndrome Coalition of the U.S. (ASC-U.S.): www.asperger.org

Programs

This is hardly a comprehensive list. Be sure to go to the Internet sites listed above for information on other programs working to include AS and NLD students. A word of caution: as NLD and Asperger's are becoming more known, some programs may be including these students without really having the knowledge or experience to provide quality programs. Be an informed consumer.

- Orion Academy, Moraga, CA. Grades 9 through 12. Currently the only high school in the country designed specifically for NLD and Asperger's students. www. orionacademy.org

- Bridges Academy, Sherman Oaks, CA. Grades 6 through 12. Gifted students with special learning needs. www.bridges. edu

- Raskob Institute, Oakland, CA. Grades 2 through 8. Designed for students with learning disabilities; the school has had experience with NLD and Asperger's. Small classes, no behavior problems.

- Star Academy, San Rafael, CA. Grades 2 through 9. Day program for AS and HFA students. Behavior issues addressed.

- Eagle Hill, Hardwick, MA. Ages 12 to 18. Residential program. www.eaglehillschool.com

- Riverview, East Sandwich, MA. Ages 11 to 22. Residential program. www.spedschools.com/schools/river.html

- CNS Pathways Academy, at McLean Hospital, Boston MA. Ages 5 to 11. Day treatment program/school with a specific focus on Asperger's, high functioning autism, and nonverbal learning disability.

Other Potential Resources for Parents

- **Coaches.** Seek licensed professionals certified as coaches with experience in life issues and organizational skills.

- **Tutors and Educational Therapists.** Local school districts or professionals in the community who work with NLD and AS students may have a list of referrals. Tutors can be most useful in helping win the "homework wars." Tutors may or may not be credentialed professionals. Some are credentialed teachers who specialize in learning disabilities and can work in specific subject matter (math, writing) or on organization in general. Other tutors are just high school or college students or interested adults in the community. Tutors without specific training as teachers can be useful for NLD and AS children, but parents must understand the limitations of their abilities. If program planning and working with the school is involved, it is likely to be a better choice to find a credentialed teacher or an educational therapist. Educational therapists are certified professionals with hours of specialized training. They can be very valuable in program development and in individual work with the child. They can reinforce what is being taught at school, act as a case manager for the child, and oversee the child's workload, helping parents who are not educational professionals understand the needs of their child.

- **Advocates.** These are people who specialize in special education law and who work with families to develop appropriate individual education plans (IEPs). In some states, there are both attorneys and nonattorneys who fill this role.

- **Occupational Therapists.** These professionals are essential members of any team that is planning a program for an NLD or AS child. An assessment by a qualified occupational therapist is a must for all NLD and AS children.

- **Speech Therapists.** A program plan for an NLD or AS child that does not include at least an assessment by a qualified speech therapist will be missing a key ingredient. Speech therapists are often the professionals most directly involved in working on pragmatic language development in these children.

It is always important to check the references of any professional you are interested in working with, making sure the person has the appropriate licenses and training as well as experience with the type of issues you are presenting. Any professional should be more than willing to give a parent the information on his or her training, experience, and license. Although confidentiality may prevent the professional from giving out names of previous clients, it should be possible to get references from other professionals in the community—doctors, teachers, or other therapists.

Appendix A: Diagnosis of NLD

Although there are no official diagnostic standards for NLD currently listed in the *Diagnostic and Statistical Manual, 4th Edition* (there are for AS), an evaluation of a child for NLD includes taking a history, performing an interview, and referring the child for testing and other evaluations. A competent assessment will produce a written report that addresses the areas of strengths and deficits found. *Specific* recommendations addressing *both* strengths and deficits should be included.

1. **Interview of the child and the parents.** A clinical psychologist, psychiatrist, or behavioral pediatrician conducts this interview, which reviews history and current functioning.

2. **Formal assessment by psychologist or neuropsychologist.** Be sure the person is licensed and has experience both with the tests listed below and with evaluating NLD and/or Asperger's children. The following tests are recommended:

   - Wechsler Intelligence Scale for Children–III (WISC-III) (ages 6 to 16). This is a test of overall intelligence that has eleven subtests, each tapping different areas. The specific scores on these subtests are more interesting for diagnosis than the overall IQ scores that are given. The subtest scores range from 2 to 19, with an average of 10. There are three IQ scores found: verbal IQ, performance IQ, and overall IQ (which actually just averages the two others). An IQ of between 90 and 110 is considered average. It is expected that there will not be more than a 12-point difference between verbal IQ and performance IQ—that the scores will be relatively similar. NLD students often show a huge difference between these scores, with verbal over performance by 20 or more points (say, a verbal IQ of 120 and a performance IQ of 95). Subtests of particular interest (Rourke 1998) for diagnosis of NLD include visual-spatial organization (object assembly, block design, and coding—not listed by Rourke, but it appears to be consistently low for NLD students); auditory perception (digit span); and language skills/general understanding of language (comprehension, vocabulary, and similarities)

- K-ABC (Kaufman) (ages 5 to 11 only). This test gives valuable information to compare to the WISC-III and offers information on learning style and on nonverbal functioning. It is not often offered, but is an excellent tool in the overall assessment.

- Vineland Adaptive Behavior Scale

- Personality Inventory for Children

- Rey-Ostereith Complex Figure Test

- Category Test

- Sentence Memory Test

- Trail Making (forms A and B)

- Specific subtests from neuropsychological assessment tools such as the Halstead Reitan: tactile form recognition; grooved pegboard; fingertip number writing; grip strength; target test.

3. **Educational assessment.** This is usually done by the school district. If your district is not qualified to assess the child's educational level adequately, seek out an educational therapist or educational psychologist. One of the two tests with a * is needed, in addition to all the others tests listed. Additional tests are often included, especially if the assessment shows area of further inquiry.

- WIAT*—all

- Woodcock Johnson*—all

- WRAT (Wide Range Achievement Test)

- Writing Sample—both sentences and paragraphs: to be evaluated for written language level

- TOWL (Test of Written Language)

4. **Occupational therapy assessment.** Refer to a qualified occupational therapist for this assessment. The assessment should evaluate sensory integration and perceptual abilities, balance, and motor skills. Specific recommendations for school and home are needed, and should include posture exercises and recommendations for desks and chairs to be used by the child.

5. **Speech therapy evaluation.** Refer to a qualified speech and language specialist. The focus of the speech therapy evaluation should be on pragmatic language, and it should include tests such as the CASL, Test of Pragmatic Language (TOPL), and a language sample in different settings, including child to adult and child to peer. The language sample evaluated by a speech and language therapist can be a very valuable tool. Use of a pragmatic language checklist of some sort (similar to the one included in this book) is an important measure of the child's functioning level.

6. **Nonverbal and social skill level.** A psychologist experienced in social skill training can evaluate the functioning level of the child's social skills. The DANVA (Diagnostic Analysis of Nonverbal Accuracy, by S. Nowicki) is a test that has been developed to evaluate the ability to read and to send nonverbal messages. It is relatively new and there are a limited number if clinicians who are familiar with it, but it may prove valuable in an overall assessment.

Appendix B: Diagnostic Criteria for Asperger's Syndrome (from DSM-IV)

A. **Qualitative impairment in social interaction, as manifested by at least two of the following:**

1. Marked impairment in the use of multiple nonverbal behaviors such as eye-to-eye gaze, facial expression, body postures, and gestures to regulate social interaction

2. Failure to develop peer relationships appropriate to developmental level

3. A lack of spontaneous seeking to share enjoyment, interests or achievements with others (e.g., by a lack of showing, bringing, or pointing out objects of interest to other people)

4. Lack of social or emotional reciprocity

B. **Restricted repetitive and stereotyped patterns of behavior, interest and activities, as manifested by at least one of the following:**

1. Encompassing preoccupation with one or more stereotyped and restricted patterns of interest that is abnormal either in intensity or focus

2. Apparently inflexible adherence to specific, nonfunctional routines or rituals

3. Stereotyped and repetitive motor mannerisms (e.g., hand or finger flapping or twisting or complex whole body movements)

4. Persistent preoccupation with parts or objects

C. The disturbance causes clinically significant impairment in social, occupational, or other important areas of functioning.

D. There is no clinically significant general delay in language (e.g., single word use by age 2 years, communicative phrases used by age 3).

E. There is no clinically significant delay in cognitive development or in the development of age appropriate self-help skills, adaptive behavior (other than social interaction), and curiosity about the environment in childhood.

F. Criteria not met for another pervasive Development Disorder or Schizophrenia.

Appendix C:
The Classroom Wish List

The contents and environment of the "ideal" classroom for an NLD or AS elementary student, presented in no particular order of importance.

- A gifted teacher with an open mind and a sense of humor, willing to learn about his or her NLD and AS students.

- A student to teacher ratio, at least during core academic subjects, of no more than twelve to one.

- A classroom that promotes kindness and tolerance of differences but is open to dealing with problems of social interactions as soon as they arise.

- A classroom that is neat and clean and uncluttered, both physically (not too much furniture crammed into a small room) and visually (the bulletin boards, whiteboards, and other teaching areas are simple and clear in their information).

- Classroom schedules that are posted and are consistent. Classroom that routines do not change without advance notice.

- A teacher who follows the schedule and routine, and who is very organized and predictable.

- Rules that are clear and consistent and consequences that are predictable.

- The availability of headphones to listen to music as needed.

- Permission to get water or go to the bathroom as needed.

- A second set of books at home to reduce remembering what needs to travel from home to school.

- The availability of technology to limit handwriting, facilitate homework transfer from home to school (using e-mail or networked classroom systems), and to improve remembering assignments. Internet access to class assignments and to the teacher.

- Classwork that uses auditory cues as often as visual cues.

- Worksheets that are not visually overwhelming.

- Models of the finished product of assignments provided for students to review before they do their assignment.

- Explicit beginning and end points of assignments; this includes help in keeping on track with reading and lectures in class.

- Teaching that explains and reviews the *main idea.*

- Homework that is not redundant.

- Projects that teach the *process* of learning, not just the concepts, and that allow the child to learn about areas of personal interest.

- A curriculum that includes social skill training as part of the overall teaching plan, not just as an adjunct program offered once or twice a week.

- Recess that has adequate adult supervision and access to supervised activities and noncompetitive games.

- Technology that is integrated into the overall program, not tacked on as an afterthought that is not understood by the staff.

- Teachers who are excited by the use of technology in their classrooms.

- Access to a challenging curriculum.

- Regular consultation for teachers and staff to review the curriculum and behavior needs of the NLD and AS students (actually, this would be great for all students).

Appendix D:
Activities for NLD Children

Martial arts. Various schools of martial arts teach self-discipline and individual success, not group successes. The rules are consistent and the practice is a good way to build strength.

Swimming. Swimming is a team sport, but the swimmers are most often only competing with themselves and their own previous times. The water provides some NLD and AS children a measure of relief from their sense of clumsiness. A note of caution: for some children the "feel" of being in the water is one of those sensory experiences they find disturbing. Early exposure and frequent access helps limit this difficulty. Never *force* a child into the water; the anxiety that results can obliterate any positive that would be gained. Encouragement and making a game of water play will be more likely to create the positive atmosphere that can develop into an interest in swimming.

Girl Scouts (and potentially Boy Scouts). As a group, Girl Scouts is supportive of differences, teaches cooperation, and offers many wonderful experiences in a supervised group. Choose the troop carefully. Look for a small troop with experienced and understanding leaders. As a parent it may be necessary for you to participate in the activities, at least in the younger grades, as an "out" for your child if the social situation becomes overwhelming. Boy Scouts has the potential to offer the same advantages as Girl Scouts—it truly depends on the leader and his or her ability to accept differences and make accommodations. The positives to be gained are many, and the experiences can help the NLD or Asperger's child develop flexibility.

4-H Club and other similar clubs. Look for groups that allow for both group and individual projects and are organized around a topic or activity of interest to the child. Many NLD and Asperger's children have a great affinity for animals and this is often a wonderful avenue for outside activities. Others prefer music or history, chess or role-playing games. If you are a parent, become involved in the child's interests. If you work at a school, try to offer opportunities for NLD and Asperger children to find a place to fit in.

Bowling. For whatever reason, this seems to be a fun activity that, although it's visual-spatial in nature, many NLD and Asperger's children enjoy. "Bumper bowling," where the gutter is filled with a bumper, is clearly preferable—though as the child gets older this may be embarrassing.

Library activities and volunteer opportunities. The library in many communities offers a wealth of activities for the elementary child that are pleasurable and quiet and that expose the child to information in an enjoyable venue. Their interest in information can develop into a volunteer or work opportunity for older children and teens.

Local animal or wildlife organizations. Animals often provide a nonjudgmental relationship for these children. Many breeds of dog, in particular, are forgiving of human social mistakes and happy to get attention from people who love them. In many areas, local animal rescue groups or wildlife area organizations have interesting activities, classes, and training opportunities. The training may lead to helper jobs, or in some cases for the teen who is ready for this, a docent job.

Appendix E:
Information Processing Deficits

Information processing deficits affect the three key areas of dysfunction in nonverbal learning disability and Asperger's syndrome. The information presented here is based on work with NLD children. It is likely that AS children are affected in a similar way, although not all aspects of these deficits affect all children in the same way. The problems that result from deficits in information processing appear to be interconnected, and the combination creates the disorder that is NLD.

Organizational Skills and Executive Function

1. Organization

- Difficulties with novel situations and learning
- Slow processing speed
- Rigid thinking
- Concrete interpretation
- Perfectionism
- Focus on the wrong detail
- Difficulty with "if-then" thinking

2. Integration

- Poor frustration tolerance: gives up easily
- Work production limited: is overwhelmed by a heavy load
- Has difficulty creating written documents
- Rigid and perfectionistic about work
- Easily overwhelmed: emotional shutdown often occurs

3. Production

- Fails to comprehend the main idea
- May see all details as equally important
- Has poor ability to understand and use metaphor and analogy
- Has difficulty reading between the lines
- Relies on pattern learning and misses concept
- Prefers a step-by-step, sequential mode of learning, often losing the whole concept

Visual-Spatial and Sensory-Motor Integration Deficit

- Is clumsy
- May not explore the world through physical activity; uses language instead
- Processes visual information slowly
- Has poor hand-to-eye coordination
- Has facial recognition problems; affects ability to read social situations
- Eye contact is often poor
- Body posture problems; limp, weak muscle tone
- Dysgraphia (difficulty producing handwriting)
- Directional confusion
- Difficulty with maintaining arousal states (attention)
- Unsure of own body boundaries
- Tactile and auditory sensitivity

Social Skills Deficits

- Difficulty writing for and interacting with the "audience"
- Difficulty taking the perspective of another person
- Often fails to conceptualize what they are talking about, losing sight of the audience's interest or comprehension
- Poor or sporadic grooming
- Poor entry into and exit from conversation
- Cognitive and behavioral rigidity
- Poor integration of multiple levels of information fields, which is required in social settings
- Difficulty predicting outcome, what would happen next
- Difficulty managing anxiety
- Does not think about how another person "feels"
- Problems with time and time references
- Trouble with novel situations
- Can't predict outcomes—which makes all interactions novel
- Experiences a limited range of feelings
- Difficulty with give-and-take in social situations
- Poor ability to understand nuances

Recommended Reading

Attwood, T. 1997. *Asperger's Syndrome: A Guide for Parents and Professionals*. London: Jessica Kingsley Publications.

Baron-Cohen, S. 1995. *Mindblindness: An Essay on Autism and Theory of Mind*. Cambridge, Mass.: MIT Press.

Cumine, V., J. Leach, and G. Stevenson. 1998. *Asperger Syndrome: A Practical Guide for Teachers*. London: David Fulton Publishers, Ltd.

Duke, M. P., S. Nowicki, and E. A. Martin. 1996. *Teaching Your Child the Language of Social Success*. Atlanta: Peachtree.

Nowicki, S., and M. P. Duke. 1992. *Helping the Child Who Doesn't Fit In*. Atlanta: Peachtree.

Rourke, B. 1998. Syndrome of Nonverbal Learning Disabilities: Assessment Protocol. NLDontheWEB.org.

Sacks, O. 1985. *The Man Who Mistook His Wife for a Hat, and Other Clinical Tales*. New York: Summit Books.

References

American Psychiatric Association. 1994. *Diagnostic and Statistical Manual of Mental Disorders, 4th Edition*. Washington, D.C.: American Psychiatric Association.

Asperger, H. 1944. Autistic Psychopathy in Childhood. Translated by Uta Frith. In U. Frith, ed., *Autism and Asperger's Syndrome*. Cambridge: Cambridge University Press.

Attwood, Tony. 1997. *Asperger's Syndrome: A Guide for Parents and Professionals*. London: Jessica Kingsley Publications.

Baron-Cohen, S. 1995. *Mindblindness: An Essay on Autism and Theory of Mind*. Cambridge, Mass.: MIT Press.

Cumine, V., J. Leach, and G. Stevenson. 1998. *Asperger Syndrome: A Practical Guide for Teachers*. London: David Fulton Publishers Ltd.

Dawson et al. 1986. Hemisperic specialization and the language abilities of autistic children. *Child Development* 57(6):1440–1453.

Duke, M. P., S. Nowicki, and E. A. Martin. 1996. *Teaching Your Child the Language of Social Success*. Atlanta: Peachtree.

Ehlers, S., and C. Gillberg. 2001. The Epidemiology of Asperger Syndrome: A Total Population Study. www.asperger.org.

Gray, C. 1994. *Comic Strip Conversations*. Arlington, Tex: Future Horizons.

Hilts, P. L. 2001. Panel Finds Earlier Autism Tests Will Lead to Better Treatment. *New York Times*, June 15, A16.

Hsu, L. 2001. Books. In *Sacred Grounds Anthology No. 6* 3(2). Oakland, Calif.: Minotaur Press.

Johnson, D., and H. Myklebust. 1971. *Learning Disabilities.* New York: Grune & Stratton.

Klin, A., F. Volkmar, S. Sparrow, D. Cicchetti, and B. Rourke. 1995. Validity and Neuropsychological Characterization of Asperger Syndrome: Convergence with Nonverbal Learning Disabilities Syndrome. *Journal Child Psychology and Psychiatry* 36(7): 1127-1140.

March, J. S., and K. Mulle. 1998. *OCD in Children and Adolescents: A Cognitive-Behavioral Treatment Manual.* New York: The Guilford Press.

Myklebust, H. 1975. Nonverbal Learning Disabilities: Assessment and Intervention. In H. R. Myklebust, ed., *Progress in Learning Disabilities*, vol. 3 New York: Grune & Stratton 85-121.

Nowicki, S., and M. P. Duke. 1992. *Helping the Child Who Doesn't Fit In.* Atlanta: Peachtree.

Rourke, B., D. Bakker, J. Fisk, and J. D. Strang. 1983. *Child Neuropsychology: An Introduction to Theory, Research, and Clinical Practice.* New York: The Guilford Press.

Rourke, B. 1989. *Nonverbal Learning Disability: The Syndrome and the Model.* New York: The Guilford Press.

———. 1995. *Syndrome of Nonverbal Learning Disability: Neurodevelopmental Manifestations.* New York: Guilford Press.

———. 1998. *Syndrome of Nonverbal Learning Disability: Assessment Protocol.* NLDontheWEB.org.

Sacks, O. 1985. *The Man Who Mistook His Wife for a Hat, and Other Clinical Tales.* New York: Summit Books.

Thompson, S. 1996. *The Source for Nonverbal Learning Disorders.* East Moline, Ill.: LinguiSystems.

U.S. Department of Education. 1999. *Office of Special Education, Annual Report.* Washington, D.C.: U.S. Department of Education.

Volkmar, F., and A. Klin. 1998. Asperger Syndrome and Nonverbal Learning Disabilities. In E. Schopler, G. Mesibov, and L. Kunec, eds., *Asperger Syndrome or High Functioning Autism?* New York: Plenum Press. 107–122.

Williams, M., and A. Shellenberger. 1994. *How Does Your Engine Run? A Leader's Guide to the ALERT Program for Sensory Regulation.* Albuquerque, N.M.: TherapyWorks, Inc.

Wing, L. 1981. Asperger's Syndrome: A Clinical Account. *Psychological Medicine* 11:115-130.

Some Other
New Harbinger Titles

Call **toll free, 1-800-748-6273,** or log on to our online bookstore at **www.newharbinger.com** to order. Have your Visa or Mastercard number ready. Or send a check for the titles you want to New Harbinger Publications, Inc., 5674 Shattuck Ave., Oakland, CA 94609. Include $4.50 for the first book and 75¢ for each additional book, to cover shipping and handling. (California residents please include appropriate sales tax.) Allow two to five weeks for delivery.

Prices subject to change without notice.